THE COMPLETE GUIDE TO
SMOKING AND SALT CURING

THE COMPLETE GUIDE TO
SMOKING AND SALT CURING

HOW TO PRESERVE MEAT, FISH, AND GAME

MONTE BURCH

Skyhorse Publishing

Skyhorse Publishing books may be purchased in bulk at special discounts for sales promotion, corporate gifts, fund-raising, or educational purposes. Special editions can also be created to specifications. For details, contact the Special Sales Department, Skyhorse Publishing, 307 West 36th Street, 11th Floor, New York, NY 10018 or info@skyhorsepublishing.com.

Skyhorse® and Skyhorse Publishing® are registered trademarks of Skyhorse Publishing, Inc.®, a Delaware corporation.

www.skyhorsepublishing.com

10 9 8 7 6 5

Library of Congress Cataloging-in-Publication Data is available on file

Cover design by Daniel Brount
Cover photo by gettyimages

Print ISBN: 978-1-5107-4531-5
Ebook ISBN: 978-1-5107-4534-6

Printed in China

CONTENTS

Preface

WHAT ONCE WAS a necessary life skill for most has become an enjoyable pastime for many. Salting and smoking meats for preservation is an age-old skill. I'm not sure my grandparents would have called salting and smoking hams and bacon a "joy"—it was a necessity of survival for them and the generations before the advent of refrigeration. I can, however, remember the fun they all had during the family and community hog-butchering days. Their skills were passed down from generations, but the skills are not hard to learn. Using smoke and salt to cure meats for preservation is a fun, easily learned process and also a great way of providing your family with great-tasting foods.

Other than cold-smoking hams and bacon, no other type of smoking or smoke cooking was done in our family when I was growing up. Later, once I discovered our home-cured hams were great slow-cooked over a rotisserie, I discovered the joy of smoking different foods and I've now been smoking meats for more than forty years. I have smoked everything from salmon to whole hogs. The delicious results are why it's no wonder the process of smoking in all forms has become increasingly popular.

In addition to salt curing, I have included both cold-smoking and hot-smoking methods in this book. I have also included some barbecuing methods utilizing smoke although there are literally thousands of recipes and entire books written on barbecue cooking.

I hope this book brings you the joy of salt curing and smoking.

PART I
About Smoking and Salt Curing

① All About Smoking and Salt Curing

SMOKING, COMBINED WITH using salt to preserve meats, is one of mankind's oldest and most important survival skills. The use of salt has a long history. Salt is one of the most important elements and was in use long before recorded history. Since the dawn of time, animals have instinctively forged trails to natural sources to satisfy their need for salt. In turn, ancient man obtained his salt from eating animal meat. As he turned to agriculture and his diet changed, he found that salt (maybe seawater) gave other foods the same salty flavor he was accustomed to in meat. Over many millennia, man learned how salt helped with preserving food. Salt was also an important trade item. Many nomadic bands carried salt with them and traded it for other goods. Wars were even fought over salt. According to the Salt Manufacturers Association (www.saltinfo.com),

About 4,700 years ago, the Chinese Png-tzao-kan-mu, one of the earliest known writings, recorded more than 40 types of salt. It described two methods of extracting and processing salt, similar to methods still in use. Writings on salt no doubt also existed on ancient clay tablets and on Egyptian papyri. Even without written evidence, we can be fairly certain that salt-making and use was a feature of life in all ancient communities.

For centuries, salt has been used to preserve foods such as meat, fish and dairy products. Even with the development of refrigeration, salt preserving remains an important aid to food hygiene. Salt acts as a binder as it helps extract the myofibrillar proteins in processed and formed meats, binding the meat together and reducing cooking losses. Used with sugar and nitrate, salt gives processed meats, such as ham, bacon and hot dogs, a more attractive color.

In addition, the use of smoke, both as a preservative and during cooking, has also been—and still is—very important. The first smoking, or "cooking," was probably done over a smudge, a smoky fire in a cave. Today smoking and smoke-cooking meats can be just about as primitive, or extremely sophisticated.

Several types of smoking can be done depending mostly on the temperature of the smoke heat applied. This includes dry or cold smoking, hot smoking, and barbecuing. Dry or cold smoking is used to impart the flavor of the smoke as well as help to dry out the meat. This is used for drying jerky and sausages, as well as for drying and adding flavor to hams, bacon, and other meats. Temperatures normally are not allowed to get above 100°F. Cold smoking is also quite often used in conjunction with the brining or salt curing of many different types of meats and meat products. All cold-smoked meats must be further cooked before consumption.

Hot smoking utilizes smoke and heat to add flavor at the same time that the meats are cooked. This type of smoking is done indirectly over hot coals, or with gas or electric heat, and temperatures rarely exceed 250°F. Cooking time is several hours. This is a common method for cooking briskets, ribs, and other popular smoked foods. Hot smoking may or may not involve water, and may be dry or moist cooking.

One of the original forms of smoke cooking is the old-time pit barbecue, and some believe the word *barbecue* comes from the Caribbean word *barbacoa*, translated as "sacred fire pit." Outdoor cooking on the barbecue grill is a very popular pastime and a favored method of cooking. In the South, *barbecue* usually refers to roast pork; in the Southwest, it usually refers to beef. Barbecuing is cooking with direct heat and may or may not include smoking. Smoking does, however, impart more flavor to barbecued foods.

In addition to salt curing, I have included both cold-smoking and hot-smoking methods in this book. I have also included some barbecuing methods utilizing smoke, although there are literally thousands of recipes and entire books written on barbecue cooking.

I'm not sure that my grandparents would have called salting and smoking hams and bacon a joy, as it was a necessity of survival for them and their parents before the advent of refrigeration. I can, however, remember the fun they all had during the family and community hog butchering days. Their skills were passed down from generations, but the skills are not hard to learn. Using smoke and salt to cure meats for preservation is a fun, easily learned process as well as a great way of serving your family great-tasting foods.

Other than cold-smoking hams and bacon, there was no other type of smoking in our family when I was growing up. Later, once I discovered that our home-cured hams were great slow-cooked over a rotisserie, I discovered the joy of smoking different foods, and I've now been smoking meats for forty years or more. I have smoked everything from salmon to whole hogs, with wonderful results. Which is why it's no wonder the process of smoking in all forms has become increasingly popular.

I hope this book brings you the joy of smoking.

THE MOST IMPORTANT tools for smoking, of course, are smokers. In days past, the smokehouse was a traditional building found on most farmsteads. These buildings often served two purposes—as a place to cure, age, and then store hams, shoulders, and other meats, as well as a place to cold-smoke them. In cold climates, the meats were usually left hanging in the smokehouse until consumed. These smokehouses varied greatly in design and size. Some were simply slats fastened to a frame; others were made of chinked

② Smokers and Other Tools

logs. Some were more elaborate and constructed to match other farm outbuildings. All, however, had a system of venting out the smoke, and many had screens over the openings to keep out pests. Sizes ranged from just a few square feet, with smoke generated in a fire outside and piped in, to larger structures capable of smoking larger numbers of hams, shoulders, and bacon. The smoke fire was built inside, either on the ground or in a stone fire pit. My granddad had such a smoke-house—one large enough to smoke the meat from a dozen or so hogs,

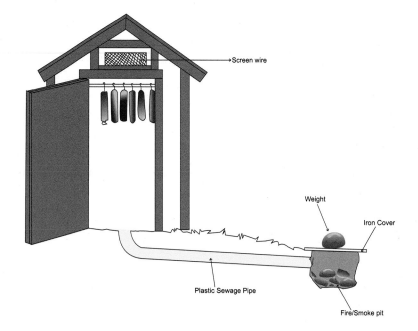

ABOVE: Smoking requires smokers, and if you intend to smoke in volume, you may wish to make up your own traditional wooden smokehouse.

as were often butchered during family and community hog butchering days. Even after he hadn't smoked in the building for years, it still held the smell of hickory smoke.

Homemade Smokers

You can build your own wooden-frame traditional smokehouse, although these days, most of us don't have the space or the need for a traditional smoke building. A better choice today is a smaller smoker. You can also make your own cold smoker quite easily. Many years ago, when I first became interested in cold smoking, I constructed my first smoker from plywood—a simple box with a door on one side, a hole on the top, and an electric hot plate holding a pan of soaked wood chips. I used the box for cold-smoking salmon and other fish, as well as some bacon.

My next smoker consisted of a fifty-gallon metal drum. I cleaned the drum thoroughly and cut out both ends. I dug a three-foot-deep and three-foot-wide hole for a fire pit, then dug a six-inch trench twelve feet long from the pit to the barrel.

It's important that the trench run slightly uphill to allow the heat-driven smoke to rise up and into the smoker barrel. I used rocks to line the fire pit, installed some six-inch stovepipe in the trench, and covered the pipe with soil. I then set the barrel in place over the end of the stovepipe. I simply placed a couple of broom-handle sticks across the barrel top, hung hams and bacon from the broomsticks, and placed the cut-off barrel top over the broom handles. I built fire in the pit, placed a metal sheet over it, and regulated the airflow by propping the metal sheet cover up or down with a rock. I placed a tarp over the barrel to create a primitive damper and to regulate smoke. This simple smoker could cold-smoke a couple of hams quite easily.

A few years later, I improved my smoker using a discarded refrigerator. As I experimented, I discovered that a refrigerator smoker can be "fired" in two ways. The first and original method was to cut a hole in the bottom or lower side of the refrigerator and install a metal stovepipe. I set this over my original stovepipe and fire pit arrange-

BELOW: A cold smoker can easily be made using a barrel or an old recycled refrigerator.

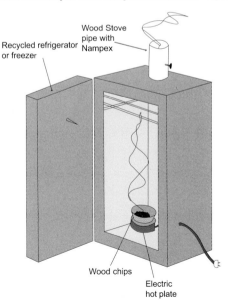

Wood Stove pipe with Nampex

Recycled refrigerator or freezer

Wood chips

Electric hot plate

ment. I cut a smoke opening in the top of the refrigerator and added a damper, a simple metal plate held in place with one screw. A wooden stove-pipe with damper could also be used. Lastly, I drilled a hole near the top of the refrigerator and installed a dial meat thermometer with silicone caulking applied around it.

The only problem with this style of smoker, as well as the smoke-houses of old, is it requires a lot of attention and effort to maintain the fire for proper cold smoking. A number of years later, I added an electric hot plate to the bottom of the refrigerator. Placing a pan of water-soaked wood chips on the hot plate made smoking easier, but it I still had to monitor the thermometer and refill the chip pan.

You can also make a propane-fueled smoker using a large barrel. This smoker can be used for both cold and hot smoking. Again the bottom is cut out and the top lid removed. Fire is provided by a cast-iron fish or turkey fryer with burner regulator.

BELOW: You can also make up your own propane-powered hot smoker using a barrel and replacement fish-fry burner and regulator.

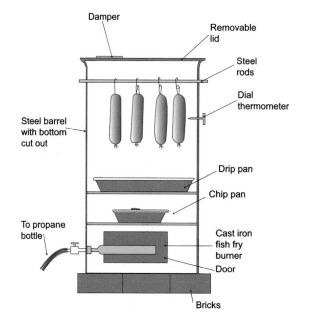

You will, of course, need racks to hold a wood chip pan, a water/grease pan, and for the meat. A dial thermometer, or a remote probe thermometer, and a damper should be placed in the top lid.

Purchased Smokers

These days smoking is extremely popular, and a number of manufactured smokers are available. They come in a wide range of sizes,

BELOW: A number of manufactured smokers are available in a wide range of types and sizes, fueled by electricity, charcoal, or wood.

styles, prices, and types of fuel used. Fuels include charcoal, wood, wood pellets, gas, and electric. The simplest to use are the electric smokers; simply plug them in and add wood chips and meat. Gas is also easy; just add wood chips and meat. The newer pellet smokers are extremely easy. Set to the desired temperature and fill the hopper with the flavor or variety of wood pellets desired.

BELOW: One of the simplest and longtime traditional smokers is the domed-lid water smoker.

Charcoal-fueled smokers require a bit more effort as well as more attention, but many prefer the taste of charcoal-smoked meats. Purist smoker chefs prefer dedicated wood smokers, but these require the most work and monitoring.

Styles include simple, water-pan, barbecue-style units; the larger dedicated indirect-heat smokers; electric-fired and gas-fired smoker/cookers; and a number of barbecue-grill smokers. Prices range from around $50 for simple domed units to several thousand dollars for smokers big enough to do a whole hog. Your first step is to determine what you want to smoke and what type of smoking you intend to do. Do you want a dedicated smoker? Do you want the convenience and ease of gas or electric, or do you prefer to smoke with charcoal or wood? How much do you want to spend? How much will you smoke at a time? Do you want to both smoke and grill? Where will you store the smoker?

The simplest and most economical are the dome-lid, water-pan smokers. Over the years, I've tested a number of these, including the Brinkmann Smoke 'n Grill, which you can find along with other brands and types of smokers at any retailer that sells smoking and barbecuing supplies. The Smoke 'n Grill is a charcoal smoker, and the style has been around for a long time.

They're economical to buy and run, and they can be used to either hot-smoke or grill. The model I've tested will grill or smoke up to fifty pounds of meat. Features include easy-to-clean porcelain-coated charcoal and water pans; a large front door for adding charcoal, wood chips, and water; two cooking racks; and a temperature gauge. Smoke cooking with water is extremely easy to do and offers a pleasant surprise if you haven't tried it. This unique cooking process combines aromatic smoke and steam to continually baste the food while the indirect heat slowly cooks it, creating delicious, succulent smoked meals. Although the unit I tested is charcoal fired, gas-fueled water cookers are also available. Most of these units can also double as barbecue grills.

Another choice is an electric smoker. These units can be used for both cold and hot smoking. Most units will run from a little over $200

These charcoal-fueled smokers utilize a pan holding water or marinades over the coals, and between the meat, providing a semi-indirect heat for long smoking times.

ABOVE: An electric smoker, such as the Bradley smoker, provides almost hassle-free smoking. Electric smokers are easy to operate and provide steady, even heat at the temperature desired, from cold to hot smoking.

to around $600. I've tested two, the Bradley and the Masterbuilt Digital models. They're very easy to operate, and they maintain a constant regulated heat. Turn them on, set to the heat desired, add the smoke materials, fill with meat, and then leave them alone. Most also have provisions for a water pan to add moistness to the cooking.

One such unit I've used for years is the Bradley smoker. Although mine is an older model, their new digital models offer a number of advantages. All models will hot-smoke at up to 320°F and cold-smoke, slow-roast, or dehydrate at 140°F.

Merely turn the thermostat to the desired temperature. One of the unique features of the units is they burn Bradley flavored bisquettes, preformed wood chip discs that self-load into the smoker.

BELOW: Bradley smokers utilize Bradley pressed-wood bisquettes to provide the smoke.

ABOVE: The smoke generator feeds bisquettes at a precise burn time of 20 minutes per bisquette.

Precise burn time is twenty minutes per bisquette. The insulated smoking cabinet is easy to use any time of the year, as I've discovered many a winter month. Six removable racks accommodate large loads and allow heat and smoke to circulate evenly. The Bradley has an easy, front-loading design. The Bradley unit also has a separate smoke generator accessory unit that fastens to the cabinet. The smoke generator can be removed and the accessory pipe used to set the smoke generator a distance from the smoker unit. Using only the smoke generator, you can create a true cold smoke at 80°F to 100°F for drying.

Probably the most versatile electric smoker I've tested is the Masterbuilt Electric Digital Smoker, which is available at most retailers. You can do anything, from simple barbecuing to cooking sausage and smoking all types of meat. The digitally controlled electric smoker comes with a remote meat probe, inside light, and a glass door.

You can actually watch your meat cook and smoke without opening the door. The push-button digital temperature and time control makes smokehouse cooking as easy as grilling. The thermostat-con-

BELOW: An accessory for the Bradley smoker sets the smoke generator a distance from the smoker, allowing for true cold smoking at 100°F or less.

ABOVE: The Masterbuilt Electric Digital Smoker is an extremely versatile electric smoker for everything from cold to hot smoking and BBQ cooking.

trolled temperature creates even, consistent smoking from 100°F to 275°F. You can easily cold-smoke or hot-smoke. The built-in meat probe helps ensure perfectly cooked food every time and instantly reads the internal temperature of the meat. Wood chips are loaded through a convenient door in the side. The Masterbuilt smoker also features a drip pan and a rear-mounted grease pan for easy cleanup. The removable pan keeps food moist. The four removable, chrome-plated cooking racks have 720.5 square inches of cooking space for large quantities of food. An air damper controls the smoke.

For true hot-smoked, barbecue-style smoking, nothing beats a dedicated indirect smoker. The better units can also be used as cold smokers. These are fueled by charcoal or wood, some newer ones by pellets. They also range in size from tailgater models to huge smokers capable of holding a whole hog. A catering friend of mine has a

BELOW: The digital controls make setting and regulating heat and time quick, easy, and precise.

ABOVE: The Masterbuilt features a removable pan for easy loading of wood chips for smoking.

BELOW: The Masterbuilt water pan provides for water smoking for hot-smoking moistness.

ABOVE: A built-in remote meat probe in the Masterbuilt provides an instant digital read-out of internal meat temperatures.

BELOW: An external drip tray makes cleanup easy.

ABOVE: The glass door on the Masterbuilt allows you to see the meat as it smokes.

ABOVE: A built-in light on the Masterbuilt makes nighttime smoking easy.

custom-made unit, on a trailer, that can smoke-cook three hogs, or a whole steer. Prices for these types of smokers begin at $600 to $700. I've also tested a number of these, wearing out a couple over the years. This is one type of smoker you do not want to scrimp on. Cheaper units are made of thinner metal, are less rigid, and simply won't last as long, as I've found out the hard way. These units, however, even the smaller ones, do require some space and are fairly heavy. They should be on a noncombustible surface such as concrete or gravel.

The 16" Horizon Classic Smoker is a fairly common size for backyard smokers, although larger units are available. The unit has the offset firebox for indirect cooking and a large cooking area that can easily smoke enough food for sixty people. Most importantly, the unit is welded from new structural steel with quarter-inch pipe. The company offers a lifetime warranty against burnout. The hinged lids are also heavy-duty quarter-inch piping. A 16" x 16" firebox provides long cooking times and fuel efficiency, and the unit will burn wood, charcoal, or a combination of both. The 16" x 32" horizontal cooking chamber has 680 square inches of available cooking surface. The side firebox door provides easy access for ash removal and damper

BELOW: An indirect, dedicated smoker, such as the Horizon, is the ultimate for serious smokers. Dedicated smokers can cold-smoke, hot-smoke, even barbecue, and they have the choice for long, low temperature or hot smoking.

ABOVE: The big firebox on the Horizon, separate from the meat-cooking area, provides plenty of space for loading lots of fuel for long cooking times.

BELOW: The Horizon smokestack with damper provides for easy regulation of heat and smoke.

ABOVE: A dial thermometer provides temperature information for easy control.

BELOW: The big cooking area on the Horizon provides lots of space for smoking for a crowd and smoking larger cuts of meat.

control. The smokestack also has a damper control. A wood storage shelf is under the cooking chamber. A grease drain and a cleanout hook make cleanup hassle-free and prevent flare-ups. Twelve-inch wagon-style wheels make the 300-pound unit easy to move around. Chrome spring handles stay cool during smoker use and last for years. A thermometer in a threaded port indicates temperature and cold- and hot-smoking ranges.

The standard and very popular barbecue grills can also be used for hot smoking. These are available in a wide range of sizes, styles, and prices from tabletop to huge built-in models. Some models can also be used for cold smoking. Models include both charcoal- and gas-fired. The larger units, or those with larger cooking surfaces,

BELOW: A standard barbecue grill, if it is large and covered, can be used for smoking. The grill must also have a temperature gauge rather than a heat range gauge.

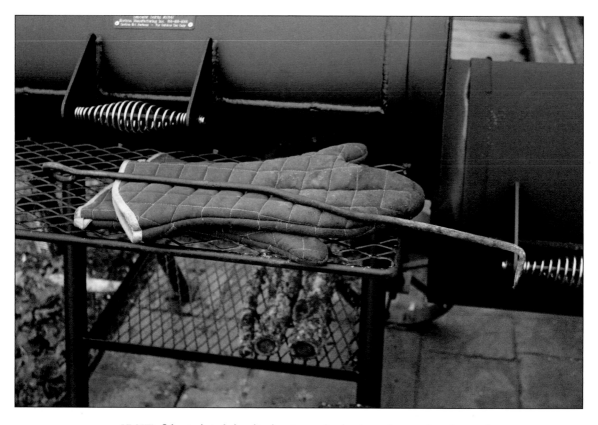

ABOVE: Other tools include a fireplace-type poker for charcoal or wood smokers, and heavy-duty insulated mitts.

are best for smoke cooking because they allow for more temperature control and indirect cooking methods.

Salt-Curing Tools

Salt-curing meats also requires some tools, the amount, number, and types depending on what kind of salt curing and smoking you do and how involved you become. If you do your own butchering, you'll need tools for those chores. Regardless, you'll need sharp knives for cutting up meat and sharpeners for keeping the knives sharp. Meat-processing or butcher knives come in a wide variety of sizes and shapes, with different types used for different chores. Wide-bladed knives are best for slicing meat into small chunks or slices. The more flexible thin-bladed knives are best for deboning meat.

I prefer the rounded-tip butcher knives for cutting meat into smaller pieces. The upswept tip doesn't "catch" on meat as you slice it. Butcher knives can be purchased separately or in sets. Some sets even include a sharpening steel as well. For instance, the RedHead Deluxe Butcher Knives Kit includes paring, boning, and butcher knives; a meat cleaver; spring shears; a square-tube saw; a honing steel; a cutting board; butcher's apron; and six pairs of gloves—all in a case.

Keeping knife blades sharp is an extremely important facet of any type of meat preparation. This is a continuous operation, and using the proper tools can make it easy to have sharp knives as needed. A wide variety of knife-sharpening devices is available, ranging from the simple but extremely effective butcher's steel to powered sharpeners. The powered hones, such as those from Chef'sChoice, can make the chore of sharpening a dull knife quick and easy.

You'll also need a work surface. It must be a good, solid surface that is easily cleaned. Salt-curing large meat cuts, such as hams and shoulders, takes quite a bit of space. Your kitchen table or kitchen

BELOW: You'll also need knives for cutting and processing meats. A variety of boning and butchering knives is a great help.

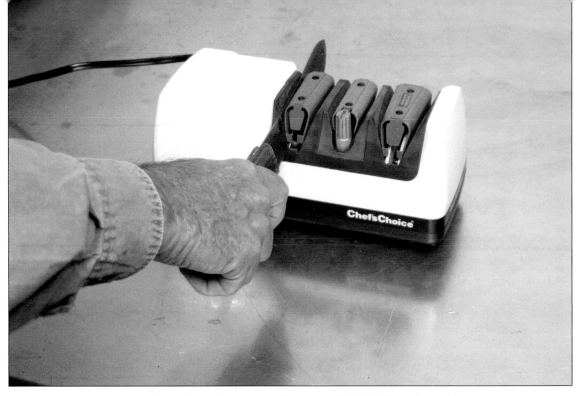

ABOVE: Keeping knives sharp is extremely important. The Chef'sChoice electric sharpeners are great for putting on a good edge and keeping knives sharp.

BELOW: A good sharpening steel, kept by the worktable, can be used for quick touch-ups.

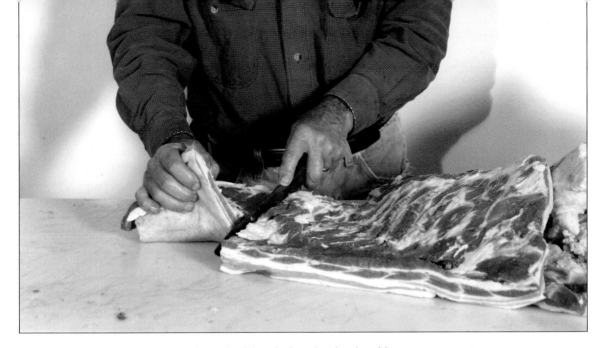

ABOVE: You'll need a good, solid, easily cleaned work surface. A large nonporous cutting board is necessary.

countertop will work, but it should not be wood, or even the traditional butcher block. The surface should be a nonporous and easy to clean and disinfect. I remember my mom using a well-kept and well-cleaned piece of "oilcloth" spread over an outside table for the chore. A very large synthetic cutting board can also be used. You'll need smaller cutting boards for cutting up the meat as well.

If you're making sausage, you'll need a meat grinder. This can be a hand-cranked or powered meat grinder. If you're doing only small batches, a hand grinder will suffice. This is economical and easy to use. Of course, hand grinders grind only as fast as your muscle power can hand-crank. With larger amounts of meat, you'll really appreciate a powered meat grinder. These are available in a number of sizes, depending on horsepower, which determines the amount of meat that can be ground in an hour.

Smaller models will do the job, but with less power, they are slower. Top models can grind up to 720 pounds per hour. The Electric Meat Grinders by LEM Products are some of the best on the market. They all feature a full two-year warranty and have heavy-duty construction featuring stainless steel, easily cleaned housing, grinder

ABOVE: If you intend to make sausage, you'll need a meat grinder. A top-quality, heavy-duty grinder such as the LEM electric grinder is the ultimate for the home meat processor.

head and auger, a permanently lubricated motor, a built-in circuit breaker, all-metal gears with roller bearings, a heavy-duty handle, and 110 V power. Standard accessories for all models include a large-capacity meat pan, a meat stomper, a stainless steel grinding knife, stainless steel stuffing plates, one stainless steel 3/16" Fine plate and one stainless steel 3/8" Coarse plate), and three stuffing tubes. Four models are available from Bass Pro. The model I tested is the no. 12, featuring a .75-horsepower motor and capable of grinding 360 pounds per hour. Sausage stuffing is what makes sausage, and a grinder with a stuffing tube makes the chore easier. For larger volumes of meat, and when using smaller-diameter stuffing tubes, you might want to go for a vertical stuffer.

You'll need a kitchen scale to weigh exact amounts of meat: 22- and 44-pound models are available at Bass Pro. The 22-pound model comes with a stainless steel tray. Other miscellaneous items include latex gloves, measuring cups and spoons, glass bowls, and a meat thermometer. A digital model with a separate temperature probe is ideal. The temperature probe can stay in the meat while the meat is in

ABOVE: A sausage stuffer, such as the LEM vertical model, makes sausage stuffing quick and easy.

the smoker. You'll also need tongs, barbecue mitts, and lots of food-grade plastic containers and bags.

BELOW: An electric meat slicer, like one of the many models available from Chef's Choice can make quick work of slicing bacon and corned beef.

AS WITH ALL types of food preparation, safety is extremely important in smoking and salt-curing meats, which requires precautions in handling meats, in preparation areas, and in storing both fresh and processed meats. The use of safe and high-quality meats is also important. Don't, however, let this take the joy out of smoking and salt curing. These processes have been in use for ages. Just follow common sense safety rules.

3

Selecting Meats and Meat Safety

Safe Meat

The first prerequisite is safe meat. Use only meat from disease-free animals, poultry, and fish. It's important to be aware of diseases, such as CWD (chronic wasting disease) found in wild deer, elk, and moose, although there is no current evidence that CWD is transmittable to humans. Health officials, however, recommend that human exposure to the CWD agent be avoided. Hunters in CWD areas are advised to completely bone out harvested cervids in the field and not consume possibly infected parts, such as the brain, eyes, spinal cord, lymph nodes, tonsils, and spleen. Do not shoot, handle, or consume any animal that is acting abnormally or appears sick. They should also take simple precautions when field-dressing, including wearing field-dressing gloves. CWD has been found in our hunting area, so during certain seasons harvested animals are required to be tested by our state (Missouri) conservation department. You can typically voluntarily get testing done by most state conservation departments

during other seasons. As a result, and following recommendations regarding handling carcasses in CWD areas, my nephew and I have developed a method to ensure safety. My nephew jokingly calls it no-gut-and-release. The carcass is not field dressed, but hung by the back legs as soon as possible. The skin is removed down to the head, then the meat boned off the hanging carcass. With a little finessing, the inside backstraps can be removed. The carcass, skin attached, guts still inside, is then disposed of. CWD areas often have regulations as to where and how you can dispose of the carcass. It's suggested where possible to leave the carcass in the general area, as transporting the carcass to other areas may spread the disease.

In our case the sample is taken and the boned-out meat frozen, labeled to the deer. So far we haven't had any positive tests and the meat thawed and smoked or cured. As suggested, wear rubber gloves and thoroughly clean knives with bleach and water. We actually take it a step further and use disposable knives for the process. Check with local authorities for regulations on carcass handling and disposal in CWD areas.

Trichinosis, or trichinellosis, is a disease caused by a parasite called *Trichinella spiralis*. It's important to avoid eating the under-cooked meat of pork, bear, cougar, wild boar, and walrus. Make sure the meat of these animals is cooked to an internal temperature of 160°F before consumption. Poultry should be cooked to an internal temperature of 165°F and fish to 160°F.

Meat that is tainted or unsafely butchered or cut up also poses serious health problems, especially from *Escherichia coli* bacteria. Food poisoning by *E. coli* is a serious and deadly problem that can make you extremely ill, even kill you. Many strains of *E. coli* exist; most are normal inhabitants of the small intestines and the colon, and are nonpathogenic. *E. coli* 0157:H7, however, is a dangerous, disease-causing bacterium from poorly cooked meat, most commonly hamburger, and the reason the disease is often called the hamburger

LEFT: Starting with safe meat is a necessity. Be aware of any possible diseases in wild animals and handle field dressing and butchering properly.

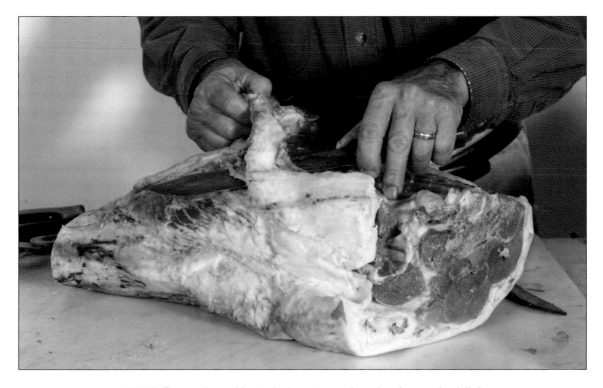

ABOVE: The meat from wild animals, domestic animals, and poultry must be chilled as quickly as possible after killing and before processing and salt curing.

disease. *E. coli* causes bloody diarrhea and cramps and blood and kidney disease in children. The most common cause of the disease is contamination of the meat from intestinal fluids, spilled or smeared on the meat during field dressing or butchering. This is especially so when the meat is then ground and the contamination is spread throughout. Although commercially butchered meat rarely carries the disease, contamination can happen. There is no reason you can't butcher your own meat as well as field-dress wild game. Just use the proper steps in field dressing and curing for the meat. If you properly process all your own meat, you will know exactly what you and your family are eating.

Regardless of whether you're using meat from wild game or domestic livestock, dress as soon as possible after the animal has been killed to allow the body heat to dissipate rapidly. Wild game, in particular, can be contaminated with fecal bacteria—the degree varying with the hunter's skill and location of the wound, among other factors. Take all the necessary steps to avoid puncturing the digestive tract, a common problem caused by not cutting around and tying off the anus during field dressing, or cutting into the intestines when opening the abdominal cavity. With a gut-shot animal, remove as much digestive material as possible and thoroughly wash out the cavity with lots of running water. Then cut away and discard any meat that has been tainted during the butchering process. Thoroughly clean and disinfect the knife before further use. Do not cut through any organs you suspect to contain disease.

Meat is a very perishable product, with deterioration beginning from the moment the animal is killed and the bleeding is done during butchering. Cool temperatures slow down the process. For this reason, most home butchering must be done in cool or cold weather. It's extremely important to rapidly chill the carcass as soon after killing as possible.

With pork to be salt-cured, this means down to 40°F, as warm meat can spoil before the salt-curing process penetrates to its center. It takes from twelve to fifteen hours to chill a 150-pound hog's carcass down to 40°F, with refrigeration or ambient air temperatures of 32°F to 35°F. Continued exposure to freezing weather, however, causes other problems with uneven chilling. Regardless of variety, if the animal is freshly slaughtered, make sure the meat is chilled rapidly and kept well chilled until it can be salt-cured, cold- or hot-smoked, or cooked.

Cleaning and Disinfecting

One of the most important facets of all steps of butchering, meat processing, salt curing, and smoking is to keep everything clean and disinfected. This includes work surfaces such as tables, countertops, and cutting boards. Make sure to thoroughly clean and disinfect knives, grinders, stuffers, smokers, grill grates, pans, as well as any tools that come into contact with the meat. Clean all surfaces with extremely hot, soapy water with a little bleach added. Then rinse with clean hot water.

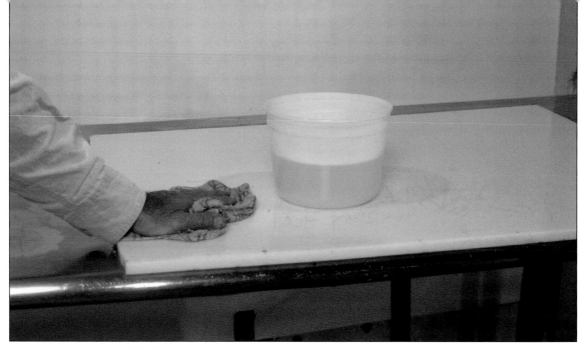

ABOVE: Keep all working surfaces and equipment clean.

BELOW: Disinfect work surfaces and equipment with a mild bleach/water solution and rinse with hot water.

A solution of bleach, soap, and water kept in a spray bottle can also be useful in cleaning surfaces and equipment. Always rinse with clean, hot water afterward. Be sure to clean and sanitize all equipment before using, after using, and before storing away. Make sure your hands and nails are scrupulously clean, or wear food-safe gloves while handling, grinding, mixing, and salting meats.

Choosing Meats

If you're using meat from a home-butchered animal, you have already controlled some of the qualities regarding how the animal, bird, or even fish is raised and then slaughtered. If purchasing meat to salt-cure, cold-smoke, hot-smoke, or cook, there are some qualities to keep in mind.

BELOW: If purchasing meats, choose only top-quality ones. Do not use freezer-burned, or possibly older, meats.

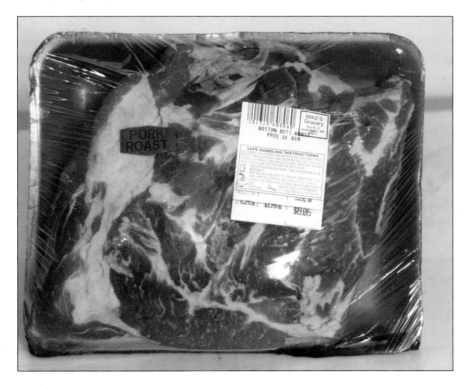

Pork

The quality of pork has changed greatly over the years. In days past, a "fat hog" for butchering often weighed 300 pounds or more, and was just that—a lot of fat. If you look at photos of the ideal hogs from several decades ago, they almost didn't have any legs, with their round, short, barrel-shaped bodies.

These days, hogs have been bred to be extremely lean, with a lot less body fat, long legs, and long frames. Most butcher hogs today are well under 300 pounds. Today's pork tenderloin is just as lean as skinless chicken breast, with 2.98 grams of fat per 3-ounce serving, meeting government guidelines for "extra lean," the reason pork is now called "the other white meat." Quality pork should have a pinkish gray lean meat with streaks of firm white fat. The meat should be fine in texture, and the outer layer of fat should be creamy white and not too thick. The skin should be smooth, free of wrinkles and hair roots. Avoid pork meat that has a coarse texture, is overly red, has white bones, and yellow fat.

Beef

Top-quality beef has a minimum of outer fat, which is creamy white in color. The bones are soft-looking and have a reddish coloration. The meat itself should be firm, fine-textured, and usually a light cherry red. Avoid beef with yellowish or grayish fat, has heavy marbling (the thicker the marble, the tougher the meat is apt to be). On the other hand, avoid beef with absolutely no marbling and with a deep red color or a two-tone coloration. Avoid beef with a coarse texture and excessive moisture, and beef that is too fresh. (Aging helps develop additional tenderness and flavor.)

Poultry

Choose poultry that is as fresh as possible. Grade A is the best poultry choice and will have nice full bodies with smooth, plump skin. Poultry should not have broken bones, bruises or discoloration, and cuts or excessively bloody areas. In many instances, you'll be purchasing prepackaged poultry products at a supermarket or store.

Make sure there are no holes or tears in the packaging. If purchasing frozen poultry, make sure there are no freezer burns and no ice crystals on the package surface. The latter indicates storage may have been less than freezing at some point. Check both the sell-by and use-by dates.

PART II
Salt Curing and Smoking

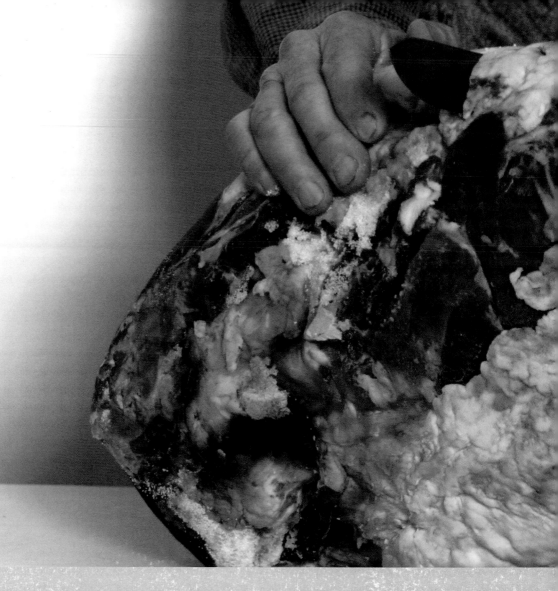

CURING MEATS WITH salt is an age-old skill. The word *sausage* comes from the Latin word *salsus*, which means salted or preserved. Sausage is preserved with salt and was a common food as far back as the Romans. Drying with cold smoke was often done to complete the preservation process as well as add flavor. A number of foods are preserved in this method. For several generations, my family has salted and cured pork hams and bacon in this method, as well as occasionally salt-curing beef. Hams treated in this manner would last a long time without refrigeration, although I have to admit, salty, dry meats are an acquired taste. These days, hams are cured and smoked

The Basics

primarily for flavor rather than preservation. Other popular salt-cured meats include bacon, salt pork, jerky, sausages, Canadian bacon, corned beef and corned venison, cured poultry, and any number of salted and smoked wild goose and fish recipes.

Salt Curing

During the curing process, the salt penetrates the meat tissue and draws out the moisture, drying the meat. The drying, as well as the concentration of salt, inhibits the growth of microorganisms. Curing agents, such as nitrate and nitrite, are also usually added.

ABOVE: These days meats are salt-cured primarily for flavor, rather than for the storage needed before refrigeration.

Although meats can be cured without the curing agents, the best results are with the agents. According to the National Center for Home Food Preservation,

> Nitrates and nitrites are curing agents required to achieve the characteristic flavor, color and stability of cured meat. Nitrate and nitrite are converted to nitric oxide by microorganisms and combine with the meat pigment myoglobin to give the cured meat color.
>
> However, more importantly, nitrite provides protection against the growth of botulism-producing organisms, acts to retard rancidity, and stabilizes the flavor of cured meat. Extreme cautions must be exercised in adding nitrate or nitrite to meat, since too much of either of these ingredients can be toxic to humans. In using these materials, never use more than called for in the recipe. A little is enough. Federal regulations permit a maximum addition of 2.75 ounces of sodium or potassium nitrate per 100 pounds of chopped meat, and 0.25 ounce sodium or potassium nitrite per 100 pounds of chopped meat. Potassium nitrate (saltpeter) was the salt historically used for curing. However, sodium nitrite

alone, or in combination with nitrate, has largely replaced the straight nitrate cure.

Since these small quantities are difficult to weigh out on most available scales, it is strongly recommended that a commercial premixed cure be used when nitrate or nitrite is called for in the recipe.

The premixes have been diluted with salt so that the small quantities which must be added can more easily be weighed. This reduces the possibility of serious error in handling pure nitrate or nitrite. Several premixes are available. Many local grocery stores stock Morton® Tender Quick® Product and other brands of premix cure. Use this premix as the salt in the recipe and it will supply the needed amount of nitrite simply and safely.

Much controversy has surrounded the use of nitrite in recent years. However, this has been settled and all sausage products produced using nitrite have been shown to be free

BELOW: Nitrites and nitrates are used to help preserve the meats and provide the characteristic coloring. Using premixed cures is the easiest method of assuring proper amounts of nitrates and nitrites in the mix.

of the known carcinogens. Remember, meats processed without nitrite are more susceptible to bacterial spoilage and flavor changes, and probably should be frozen until used.

Nitrates and nitrites, supplied by potassium nitrate (saltpeter) and Prague powder, have traditionally been used to aid in curing meats. You can purchase the curing ingredients separately and make up your own blend following any number of recipes, or you can purchase premixed, ready-to-use cures and seasonings, with "guaranteed" results. The latter are available from a wide range of butcher supply companies, many on the Internet. Morton Salt's curing products are a longtime favorite for home meat curing and have been used by my family for many years. The Morton Salt family of curing products includes Morton Tender Quick mix, a fast-cure product that has been developed as a cure for meat, poultry, game, salmon, shad, and sablefish. It is a combination of high-grade salt and other quality curing ingredients that can be used for both dry and sweet-pickle curing. Morton Tender Quick mix contains salt, the main preserving agent; sugar; both sodium nitrate and sodium nitrite (curing agents that also contribute to the development of color and flavor); and propylene glycol, to keep the mixture uniform. It can be used interchangeably with Morton Sugar Cure (Plain) mix. It is not a meat tenderizer. Morton Sugar Cure (Plain) mix is formulated for dry or sweet-pickle curing of meat, poultry, game, salmon, shad, and sablefish. It contains salt, propylene glycol, sodium nitrate and sodium nitrite, a blend of natural spices, and dextrose (corn sugar). The *Morton Salt Home Meat Curing Guide* advises,

> Caution: These curing salts are designed to be used at the rate specified in the formulation or recipe. They should not be used at higher levels as results will be inconsistent, cured meats too salty, and the finished products may be unsatisfactory. The curing salts should only be used in meat, poultry, game, salmon, shad and sablefish. Curing salts should not

be substituted for regular salt in other food recipes. Always keep meat refrigerated (36° to 40°F) while curing.

The spices used in Morton Sugar Cure (Plain) mix are packaged separately from the other ingredients. This is to prevent any chemical change that may occur when certain spices and the curing agents are in contact with each other for an extended period of time. If you do not need an entire package of Morton Sugar Cure (Plain) mix for a particular recipe or must make more than one application, prepare a smaller amount by blending 1 ¼ teaspoons of the accompanying spice mix with 1 cup of Morton Sugar Cure (Plain) mix. If any portion of the complete mix with spice is not used within a few days, it should be discarded. It is not necessary to mix the spices with the cure mix if spices are not desired. The Morton Sugar Cure (Plain) mix contains the curing agents and may be used alone. Morton Smoke Flavored Sugar Cure mix is formulated only for dry-curing large cuts of meat, such as hams or bacon. It contains salt, sugar, sodium nitrate, propylene glycol, caramel color, natural hickory smoke flavor, a blend of natural spices, and dextrose (corn sugar). The cure reaction takes longer with this mix than with the Morton Sugar Cure (Plain) mix, so the smoke-flavored product should be used only for dry curing, and is not for making a brine (pickle) solution. The Morton Sausage & Meat Loaf Seasoning Mix is not a curing salt. It is a blend of spices and salt that imparts a delicious flavor to a number of foods. The seasoning mix can be added to sausage, poultry dressing, meat loaf, and casserole dishes, or it can be rubbed on pork, beef, lamb, and poultry before cooking.

Other cure and seasoning mixes are also available. The Sausage Maker carries Maple Ham or Bacon Cure, Honey Ham or Bacon Cure, Country Brown Sugar Cure, as well as Corned Beef Cure. A complete meat-curing kit includes netting, bacon hanger, brine tester, baby dial thermometer, meat pump, stockinette hooks and Honey Ham Bacon Cure, Maple Ham or Bacon Cure, Brown Sugar Cure, Insta Cure No. 1, and a 5-gallon brining bucket.

LEM Products carries a number of cures for pork as well as venison, including Bacon Cure, dry rub; Venison Bacon Cure, dry rub; Bacon Cure, smoked wet brine; and Venison Bacon Cure, smoked wet brine. Also available from the company are their Backwoods Ham Curing kit and injector. The kits come with Sweeter than Sweet Ham Cure or Brown Sugar Ham kit, which includes two nets for hanging the ham, meat injector for injecting the ham, and complete instructions.

Bradley Smoker has Demerara Cure, Honey Cure, Maple Cure, and Sugar Cure. Hi Mountain Seasonings has their Alaskan Salmon Brine, Buckboard Bacon Cure, Game Bird or Poultry Brine Mix, Gourmet Fish Brine, and Wild River Trout Brine. From Sausage Source come the Luhr-Jensen Brine Mixes.

You can, of course, make up your own cure mixes. Use only pickling or canning salt when making up a cure, and never use iodized table salt. Salt used alone produces a harsh, sometimes bitter taste. For this reason, sugar, as well as spices, is added for flavor. A wide range of spices can be used for the various cured meats. Most of these are available at your local grocery, but some may need to be purchased from butcher-supply houses. Fresh spices are the best, as they add the most taste.

BELOW: A number of premixed cures are available almost anywhere.

ABOVE: You can, of course, make up your own brine cures. Use only pickling or canning salt.

Many spices lose their flavor over time, especially if kept longer than six months at room temperature. Best storage for spices and seasonings is below 55°F in airtight containers. Grinding your own fresh spices is the best method for getting the freshest flavor.

General Curing Methods

Meats may be cured using several methods, as well as a combination of methods. These methods include dry curing; pickle, liquid, or immersion curing; and pump curing. Each has its advantages and disadvantages. The old, traditional method of home curing is dry curing, or rubbing the salt and curing agents onto the surface of the meat. This is the method my family has used for generations to cure

ABOVE: The traditional method of salt curing is with a dry rub.

hams and bacon. A dry sugar cure is the easiest to do—less chance of spoilage, can be done in a wider range of temperatures, and the product is generally less perishable. There is more flavor, but also more of a harsh, salty taste. Pickle, or immersion curing, utilizes a salt cure dissolved in water, and the meat is immersed in liquid.

This method is slower; the solution has to be changed every seven days to prevent spoilage, and a salimeter must be used to ensure the salt strength or salinity of the cure pickle is correct. This method has generally been replaced by pump pickling, or pumping the pickle into the meat. The best method for larger cuts such as hams is to use a combination of pumping the hams with the pickle solution and rubbing on the dry cure.

The traditional recipe for dry curing is an 8-3-3 mixture—using 8 pounds of salt, 3 pounds of sugar, and 3 ounces of saltpeter. Another time-tested, less-salty recipe is 5 pounds of salt, 3 pounds of brown or white sugar, 2 ¾ ounces of sodium nitrate, and ¼ ounce of sodium nitrite (or a total of 3 ounces of nitrate available). Again, do not use more nitrite, as it is toxic. Use 1 ounce of the cure per 1 pound of meat. In our family recipe, we never used saltpeter, nitrate, or nitrites; and the ham was always a gray color. Our hams were traditionally cured, then aged, country-style; and black pepper was also used to help prevent insect infestations during the aging process.

An old-time pickle solution consisted of 8 pounds of salt, 2 pounds of sugar, and 2 ounces of saltpeter dissolved in 4 ½ gallons of water. The pickle solution was used to immerse the meat.

BELOW: In some cases a pickle cure is used.

Cold Smoking Techniques

Smoking, often combined with salt curing to dry and preserve meats, is one of mankind's oldest and most important skills. In addition, cooking with smoke has also been, and still is, very popular today. As I have said in chapter 1, the smoke-cooking methods today can either be olden-days primitive or modern-day sophisticated.

First, you must understand the process of smoking. Several types of smoking can be used, depending mostly on the temperature of the heat applied. These include dry or cold smoking and two types of hot smoking, indirect heat and direct heat. Dry or cold smoking is used mostly to help dry out the food and also to impart the flavor of the smoke into the food. This is primarily used for drying jerky and sausages, as well as for drying and adding flavor to hams, bacon, and sometimes fish. Any number of methods and smokers can be used to cold-smoke the meats. In cold smoking, the majority of the heat is kept away from the meat; only the smoke is used. In days past, wooden

BELOW: Salt-cured meats are often cold-smoked for further flavor, to add color and to aid preservation.

smokehouses, such as the one on my granddad's farm, were used to create the cold smoke used for hams and bacon. Some of today's purchased smokers can also create the needed cold smoke, or you can construct your own backyard cold smoker. The Bradley smoker, with its cold-smoke accessory, is an ideal home cold smoker. Cold smoking is typically a long affair, requiring lots of attention to the chore; but with newer types of smokers, the time is greatly shortened.

There are so many variables in cold smoking that it is not really an exact science. Each fish, fowl, or piece of meat is somewhat different in moisture content, as well as the moisture in the air. It's to your advantage to keep good records of what you smoked, how much it weighed, the amount and type of brining used, and the proper amount of smoking for the end result. Smoking can be as simple or complicated as you like. Primitive people merely used a cured animal skin draped over a framework of saplings and a small smoldering fire.

The following method was used by my family for many years to smoke hams and bacon: Soak the cured meat for about a half hour in cold, fresh water. Use a heavy string to make loops for hanging meat in the smokehouse. Hams and shoulders should be tied through the shank. Light pieces, such as bacon, should be reinforced with wooden skewers. After stringing, scrub the meat clean with hot water and a stiff brush. The water should be about 110°F to 125°F. Then hang the meat up and let it dry. If you don't scrub the meat clean and allow it to dry thoroughly, the smoke won't take evenly, and the meat will be streaked in appearance. The meat should hang overnight in a cool, safe place.

Carefully hang the meat in the smokehouse so none of the pieces are touching. Build a fire in the pit using a hardwood, such as oak, hickory, or apple, or even corncobs. Place a thermometer in the smokehouse and allow the smokehouse to heat up to 100°F, or just hot enough to begin to melt the surface fat on the pork. Then open the top ventilator of the smokehouse just a bit to let out moisture. On the second day, close the ventilator and continue to smoke for at least one more day, or until the meat takes on the desired color. You don't need a dense cloud of smoke—a slight haze will work just as well. The most important thing is not to overheat and cook the meat after the initial start-up—remember you're cold smoking the meat.

The best type of fire in the pit is one built in the Indian fashion of sticks radiating out from the center of a wheel. As the sticks burn, you can continue to push the sticks into the center and add more wood. This type of fire will become cooler and lower rather than hotter as it burns. You can also use twigs or green sawdust to dampen a fire and make it smoke better. One of the main problems with cold smoking is inattention to the fire and the ruined meat in the smokehouse. This takes time and attention. You also need cool to cold ambient temperatures. Smoke only until you achieve the desired nut-brown coloration. Some old-timers in the Ozarks butchered hogs in the early winter, cured and aged the meat until early spring, and then smoked the hams. The bacon was usually already consumed by the time the hams were ready to be smoked.

Using these old ways doesn't always guarantee results. At the end of the smoking period, run a clean, stiff wire into the meat. It should be run in along the bone to the center of the ham and then withdrawn. If it has a sour odor, the meat is tainted. If it doesn't have a sour odor and smells "sweet," the meat is sound. If you get a tainted odor, cut open the meat and examine it for spoilage. If the meat gives off a definite odor of putrefaction, you'll have to discard the entire piece. About the only time I remember my grandfather in a sweat, no pun intended, was when he was waiting for the meat to come out of the smokehouse. In those days of no refrigeration, the smoked meat was really valuable. These days, however, cold smoking of meats is normally done for much shorter times, under more controlled circumstances, and only to add flavor to the meats.

Cold smoking is usually done at 80°F to 100°F. Cold-smoked foods must be further cooked or heat-treated in some means to kill pathogens, the temperature depending on the meat. This may be by conventional oven or by using hot-smoking or smoke-cooking methods. Part III covers hot smoking or smoke cooking of all types of foods, including cold-smoked foods.

EARLY SETTLERS TRADITIONALLY relied on pork
for a great deal of their domestic meat. Pigs were economical, fast to
grow, and easy to feed. In many instances, the hogs were simply turned
out in the woods to fatten on acorn mast. Pigs are also very prolific,
providing a lot of meat in a hurry. With an abundance of meat, a means
of preservation for extended use became necessary. During the early
times, and even today, pork is one of the most popular meats for salt
curing and smoking. These pork meats include hams, picnic hams,
bacon, Canadian bacon, jowls, and, a necessity for early seafarers

⑤ Pork

as well as trappers and explorers, simple salt pork. Pork sausage is another common salt-cured meat.

Hog butchering days were a tradition in our family, with the entire community coming in for the chore. A dozen or more hogs might be butchered during the day by several families. I remember butchering day as great fun, with lots of excitement. Even the adults seemed to have fun, despite the work. Curing your own pork can still be fun, and a great way of preserving and enjoying a traditional American food.

Curing Ham

Ham is one of the most popular pork cuts for curing. Curing a ham takes some skill, but it is easily learned. Hams can be cured with a homemade recipe or using a purchased cure. The latter contains the proper amounts of nitrites and nitrates, and in some cases, the seasonings as well, making the job easier and the results more consistent. A number of these commercial cures are easily available.

Hams are available in several different types, including fresh or noncured; regular cured; aged, or country-style; and picnic. Hams may or may not be smoked, and they can be cured with different seasonings for a variety of tastes. The first step is to decide what type of ham you wish to cure. How you cut or trim the meat is the first determining factor. The two most common types are the short-cut (regular) ham and the long-cut (country-style) ham.

A short-cut ham is the type most commonly found in grocery stores. It has not been aged and may or may not be smoked. Less salt is used, and the curing time is shorter, creating a milder-tasting product. A long-cut ham is used to make the aged or country-style ham, sometimes called a Virginia or Smithfield ham. A picnic ham is made from the front shoulder of the hog, which is usually smaller. Boneless hams are also very popular, and you can create them as well.

To create a short-cut ham, make the cut separating the ham from the pork side, between the second and third sacral vertebrae, or halfway between the pelvic arch and the end of the pelvic bone. This

BELOW: Hams are cut in two methods, depending on the curing methods, short cut (regular) and long cut (for aged hams).

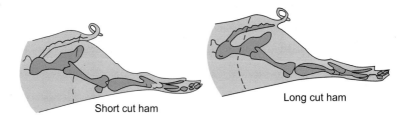

Short cut ham

Long cut ham

exposes an open end of the shank bone. Trim the ham by cutting off the first five to six inches of skin from the butt end to about half the distance to the hock end. Cut away excess fat, leaving about one-half inch thick at the butt end.

A long-cut ham to be aged is cut perpendicular to the side and at the pelvic arch, or the bend in the back. This keeps the shank bone intact—with no sponge bone, or marrow, exposed—and provides greater protection from bone souring and from bacteria entering the ham during the aging process. Remove the tail, but leave the skin attached to protect from insects during aging. Excess fat should be removed for proper cure penetration. There will be a slight protrusion of the aitchbone, and this should be sawn off so curing agents can be worked well around the butt end of the ham. Trim up rough corners to smooth and round the ham.

BELOW: Remove the hock.

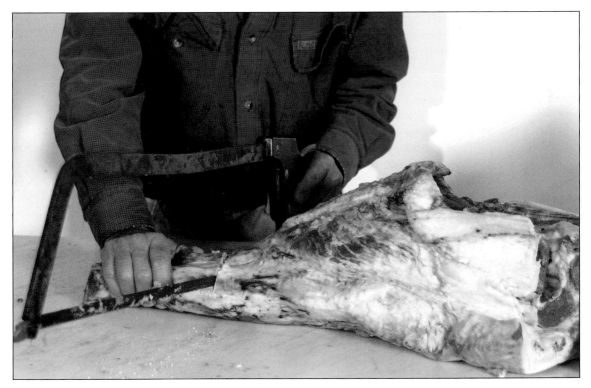

ABOVE: Cut to create the size of ham desired.

BELOW: Trim away excess fat and smooth up the ham.

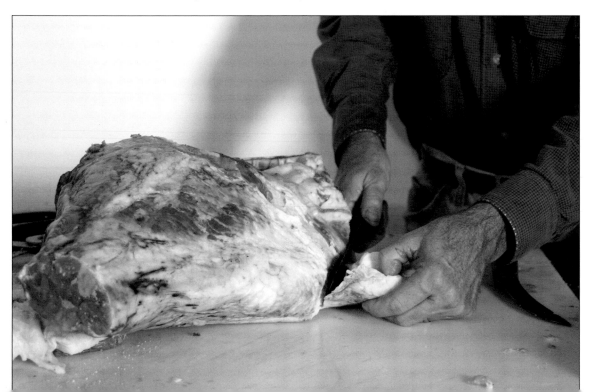

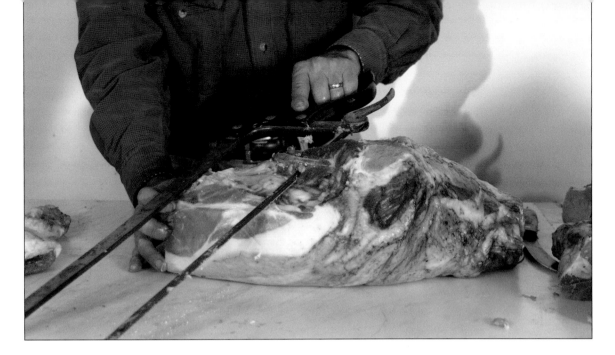

ABOVE: Trim the aitchbone for long-cut hams.

BELOW: The resulting long-cut ham is ready for curing into an aged ham.

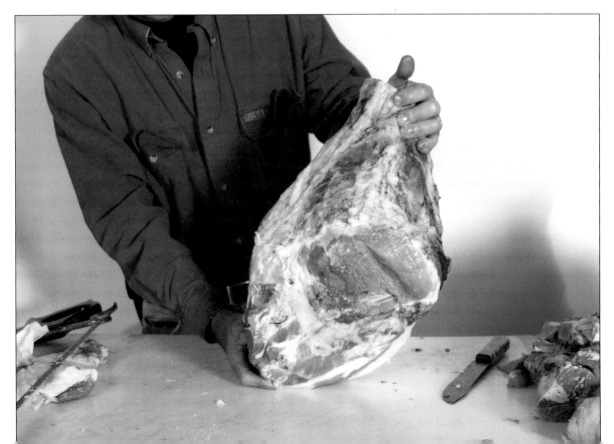

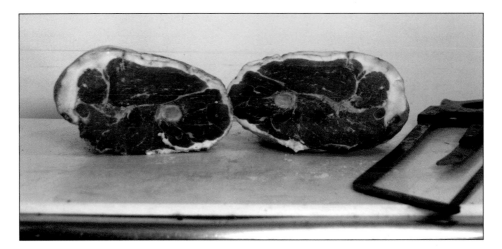

ABOVE: Hams can also be short cut for regular curing.

You can also make a boneless ham, and this is the best tactic for hams weighing more than 25 pounds. Position the ham skin-side down and with the butt end facing you. Using a boning knife, remove the meat from around the aitchbone. Disjoint the aitchbone from the straight long leg bone. Cutting through the top of the ham, remove the leg and shank bone intact, turning the boning knife to trim around the bones as you lift them out. With all bones removed, shape the ham into a roll and tie with white butcher's string. Space the ties crosswise about an inch apart. The boneless roll is treated and cured as for a regular ham.

Hams may be cured using three different processes—dry cure, wet or immersion cure, and the combination cure.

Dry Cure

Dry curing is the traditional and most popular method. Weigh the ham and mix your own cure, or obtain the proper amount of prepackaged cure. Dry-cure hams are cured by rubbing the cure over and into the meat, sometimes with only one application. Other recipes, however, require two to three separate applications. Short-cut, picnic, and long-cut hams require different amounts of cure, different numbers of applications, and different curing times between

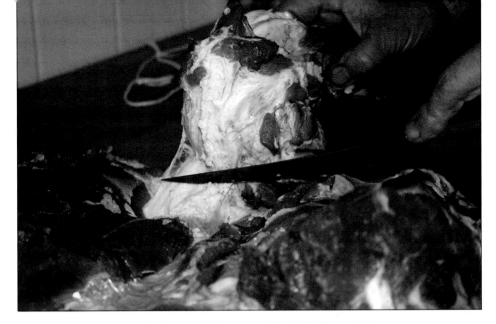

ABOVE: You can also bone out the ham, using a thin-bladed boning knife.

applications. A general method is to use three separate rubbings at intervals of three to five days. Picnic hams require only two rubbings, and some aged ham recipes call for only one application.

Divide the cure mixture into two, three, or a single portion, depending on the number of applications. For use with their Tender Quick or Sugar Cure, Morton Salt suggests ¾ ounce (1 ½ tablespoons) for each pound of meat. If the ham is long-cut and to be aged, use 1 to

BELOW: Dry curing is the traditional method of curing a ham. Morton Salt Sugar Cure is used here.

ABOVE: Or you can make up your own cure mix.

1 ¼ ounces (2 to 2 ½ tablespoons) of curing mix per pound of meat. Measure the cures and have the portions ready to apply before you start working on the ham. Make sure the ham is kept well chilled. Apply the first portion as quickly as the ham can be prepared. Apply the second portion three to five days after the first.

Then for long-cut hams to be aged, make a third application, ten to fourteen days after the first. When rubbing in the cure, make sure all surfaces are well covered, especially the ends. Work the cure in well around the bone ends. Position the ham with the flesh-side up and apply any excess cure on this side.

During the curing process, the ham should be kept at temperatures between 34°F and 40°F. This will usually be in a refrigerator, although some may have access to a cold storage unit. If cold storage space isn't available, you must cure in cold weather. Because of this temperature requirement, we always butchered in late winter in Missouri, as the winter temperature is normally cold and fairly consistent at that time.

To cure, the meat must be placed in a noncorrosive pan or container, or in double-lined plastic food-storage bags. Use only food-storage bags—not nonfood plastic products or garbage bags, as they may contaminate the meat. Position the ham skin-side down on a tray and place in a refrigerator.

The length of curing time for a ham depends on its size as well as the ham type. The common method for dry-curing long-cut hams is 7 days per inch of thickness, or two days per pound. A ham that weighs 16 to 18 pounds and is approximately 5 inches thick at the thickest portion would need to cure for about 35 days. Hams that are short-cut, partially skinned and/or cured using a combination, can

BELOW: Weigh the ham.

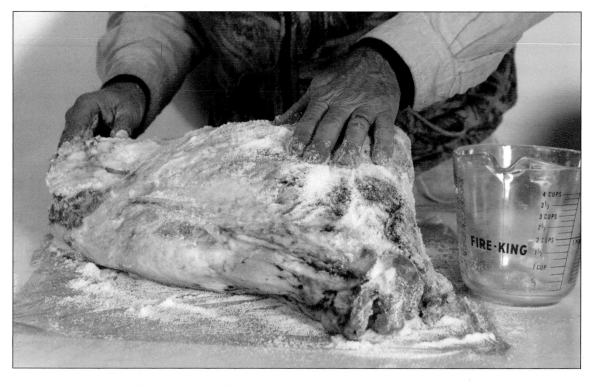

ABOVE: Coat the ham well on all sides with the dry cure mix.

be cured at 5 days per inch or 1 ½ days per pound. Don't guess at the cure application dates or curing time. Mark the timing and dates on a calendar posted nearby or on the bag or container.

Immersion Pickle Cure

Immersion or pickle curing is a bit more complicated. The process is slower, and the pickle must be changed every 7 days to prevent spoilage. In the old days, pickling was a common method of curing bits and pieces of pork for salt pork that was used for flavoring and cooking other foods. These days, immersion curing is more precise. A salinity of 75 to 85 percent is suggested, as determined by a salimeter. The percentage must be tested with the water at 60°F, and without the addition of sugar or phosphates. Pickle-curing time for meats immersed in the brine is approximately 3 ½ to 4 days per pound of ham, or 11 days per inch of thickness, measured at the thickest portion through the center of the ham. For instance, a 15-pound ham would take up to 60 days to cure with the immersion method.

Injection pickle curing speeds up the immersion process with a more complete distribution of the curing liquid into the center of the meat. A portion of the brine is pumped or injected into the meat using two methods: stitch or artery. In the stitch method, a perforated needle is used to inject the cure. In the arterial or artery method, the pickle is pumped directly through the femoral artery of the ham. The pickle should be pumped into the ham at a rate of 10 percent of its weight. A ham weighing 15 pounds requires 1.5 pounds of pickle. Place the meat on a scale during the pumping process to determine when the correct amount has been applied.

BELOW: Place the ham in a large food plastic container or large food bag and place in the refrigerator to cure.

Combination Cure

The best method is the combination cure. This combines pumping the ham with a pickling cure along with rubbing the dry cure mix onto the surface of the meat. With the combination method the cures work from both inside and outside the meat. This makes the meat inside, near the bone, cure more rapidly than with dry-cure alone, thus reducing the chance of spoilage from bone-sour. The remainder of the ham, cured in the traditional dry-cure method, also cures more evenly. And curing time is shortened to about one-third. The combination cure is the preferred method recommended by Morton Salt with their products, and they say, "When used properly, success is almost guaranteed."

The first step is to weigh the ham to determine how much pickle and dry cure mixes to prepare. Prepare a pickle cure by combining one cup of Morton Sugar Cure (Plain) mix or Morton Tender Quick with four cups of water and stir until thoroughly dissolved. Pump the ham with one ounce of pickle cure per pound of meat. If using a Morton Salt pump, four pumps will utilize 16 ounces of pickle cure.

It's important to properly pump the meat. Make sure the meat pump is full to avoid forming air pockets in the meat. Insert the needle to its full length into the meat. Slowly push the pump handle with an even pressure to inject the pickle into the meat near the bone. Slowly and gradually withdraw the needle as you finish the injection, to distribute the cure evenly.

The diagrams of a ham and shoulder show the bone structure. The numbered lines indicate locations where the needle of the meat pump should be inserted into a large ham or a shoulder for five different pumping strokes. If a ham or shoulder is small, eliminate strokes numbered 4 and 5.

Once you have pumped the pickle in place, the Morton Salt dry-cure is applied. The amount of curing mix applied depends on the size of the ham, along with the curing method chosen. "If the hams will be aged, use ¾ to 1 ounce (1 ½ to 2 tablespoons) of curing mix for each pound of meat. If the ham will not be aged, use ½ ounce (1 tablespoon) per pound of meat." Once you've measured out the proper

ABOVE: Injecting a pickle cure, along with the dry cure or a combination cure is the best method of curing a ham.

amount of cure, divide it in half and apply half to the ham surface. Five to seven days later, apply the other half of the cure to the ham surface. This allows the cure to penetrate the meat more evenly.

Spices are not required for a successful cure, as the curing agents, sodium nitrate and sodium nitrite are included in the Morton Salt cure. Spices are included in a separate packet and can be used, mixing them into the cure mix just before application.

Using half of the measured cure mix to be applied, sprinkle the mix on the skin side of the ham and rub it in thoroughly. Turn the ham over, apply the other portion to the meat side, and rub it in well. Make sure to work plenty of the cure mix into both the shank and butt ends and work around any exposed bones. Scoop up and pile any of the surplus cure onto the meat side of the ham.

Again, the combination-cured ham should be cured for about two-thirds of the time needed for a dry-cured ham. After the initial cure, the ham must undergo an equalization period, regardless of whether a dry or a combination cure was used. This allows the salt to further penetrate and spread more evenly throughout the meat to help preserve the ham. If the ham is to be aged, the entire ham should have a salt content of at least 4 percent. If this is achieved, the ham will not spoil or sour, even if temperatures reach as high as 100°F.

For the equalization period, the cured ham should be placed in a tub of clean, cool water and allowed to soak for an hour. This helps to dissolve the curing mix on the surface, distributing the seasoning more evenly. Lightly scrub excess cure from the surface and pat the ham dry. Place the ham into a large clean plastic food bag and return it to the refrigerator for the equalization period. For combination cures, this will take 14 to 15 days; for dry-cured hams, 20 to 25 days. Because the curing agents or salts have been removed from the ham's surface, bacteria may grow there, causing it to become slimy. To help prevent this, keep the bag partially open. This slime growth, however, is not harmful and can be washed or scraped off after the equalization period. A bit of vinegar helps to wash off the mold. After this period, the ham should have shrunk approximately 8 to 10 percent. A short-cut, or regular, ham is now ready to cook and eat or wrap and store in the freezer.

Country Ham Cure

The traditional country, Virginia- or Smithfield-type, aged hams were a staple of the early settlers as these could be stored almost indefinitely. My ancestors were from Virginia, and the hams my grandparents preserved were also aged Virginia-style. Country-style ham has a very different and distinct flavor—very salty, somewhat pungent, and definitely an acquired taste. But the flavor is hard to beat when it's fried for breakfast and served with redeye gravy. A country ham requires additional steps, including aging and smoking if desired.

Some folks like to smoke the ham first and then age, but smoking can destroy some of the enzymes. The flavor and aroma of aged hams come through enzymatic action created by aging the meat in warm weather from 45 to 180 days. Like aging wine or cheese, the flavor comes from the aging process, and is both an art and a science. You'll

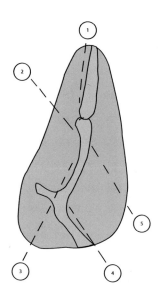

ABOVE: Using a meat pump, inject the pickle along the bone and in the areas shown.

probably have to experiment a bit until you get the results you desire. The best weather conditions for aging are 75°F to 90°F, and with a relative humidity of 55 to 65 percent. At temperatures over 95°F, the flavor may not develop properly, which is another reason many countrypeople butchered in December. Not only is the cold weather required to properly chill the meat during slaughter and then cure it properly before it spoils, but spring also offers the right conditions for aging the hams. Aged properly, the ham may lose 8 to 12 percent of initial weight during the process. Before aging, many experts like to recoat the hams to create special flavors. Coatings may include black pepper, molasses, brown sugar, and/or cayenne pepper. The hams should be wrapped with paper, such as plain brown paper, then placed in muslin sacks and hung in a cool, dry area with lots of good air circulation. A drafty old barn used to be a popular location. Do not use plastic bags, plastic wrap, or waxed paper that may not allow for air circulation, and do not age in an airtight room.

Another method is also popular for country-curing hams, and is the method used by our family for generations. We basically elimi-nate the equalization period, wrapping and hanging the hams to cure

ABOVE: A traditional country-cure ham is typically cured with a dry rub.

and age naturally in the Missouri winter, spring, and summer weathers. Another reason is that in the old days, we didn't have the space to cure in the refrigerator. Hams should not, however, be placed outside to cure after January, or in warmer climates. Hams need to cure at least 35 to 45 days with a temperature less than 40°F to prevent spoilage. If freezing occurs during the curing time, allow one additional day for each day/night the temperature drops below freezing.

Burch Family Sugar Cure Recipe

2 cups of salt	4 tbsp. black pepper
I cup brown sugar	2 tbsp. red or cayenne pepper

Apply at the rate of 1 ¼ ounces per pound of ham.

Lay out brown paper, paper bags or brown wrapping paper, on a clean flat surface. (We have used newspapers for years, but do not use paper with colored inks.) Place the ham on the paper skin-side up and spread the cure mix over the skin. Force some of the cure into the open end of the cut hock. Make sure all surfaces are well covered.

Gently turn the ham over, being careful not to knock off the cure. Coat the cut or flesh side well with the remaining cure mix. Make sure to work the cure well around the cut side and shank end. Work the mix well into the area around the end of the shank bone.

BELOW: Place the ham on clean brown wrapping paper or spread out paper bags or black-and-white newspaper. Cover the ham on all sides with the dry cure, making sure the cure is rubbed well into the joints.

Carefully wrap the paper up around the ham and, holding the paper in place, slide a rectangular homemade muslin bag or purchased stockinette over the paper-wrapped ham. Place the ham in the bag with the shank pointing down to one corner of the bag. Pull the bag tight around the ham and use a stainless steel safety pin to hold it in place. Tie a knot in the bag or tie a heavy cord around the end of the bag.

Allow the bagged ham to sit in place on the table, if it is safe from varmints, for a day to allow the cure to become wetted by the ham liquids. This helps to hold the cure in place.

Hang the ham in a well-ventilated, dry area, again with the shank down, to allow for drainage. The ham will drain, so don't place it over anything that will be damaged by the salty liquid. Do not hang in a moist area with little ventilation, such as a basement or root cellar. If you begin in December, the ham should be cured around the first of April.

You can clean and process the ham for equalization. Then the aging process begins, and the hams can be aged from three to six months. If the hams are in a well-ventilated area, they can also simply be left wrapped from the cure throughout the aging period. This is the method our family has been using. We hang our hams from rafters in an old smokehouse or the barn. We make sure they are well wrapped, and we've never had any insect infestation. It is a good idea to check the hams once a month to make sure rodents or insects have not chewed their way into the hams. Unprotected or stored improperly, ham may be damaged by a number of insect pests, including blowflies, ham mites, cheese or ham skippers, as well as a number of ham beetles.

Smoking

Smoking the ham is not necessary for preservation. Smoking, however, adds to its dark-mahogany appearance, as well as its flavor and preservation. As stated before, you can smoke after curing and before aging, or after aging. Some Smithfield-style hams are smoked after curing, but before aging. Regardless, remove the ham from the

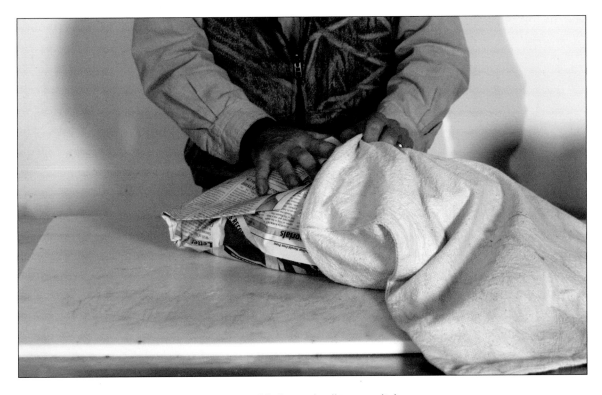

ABOVE: Wrap the paper up around the ham and stuff into a muslin bag.

bag and wash off all mold growth using a stiff brush and cold water. Pat the ham dry and allow it to hang in the smokehouse or smoker for an hour or two to dry thoroughly. The hams must be smoked with a cold smoke not exceeding 85°F to 100°F. Use only hardwood logs, chips, or sawdust to create a smoldering fire. If smoking more than one ham, make sure that they do not touch each other. Smoke until the hams achieve the color you desire. This will take from 1 to 3 days.

A properly cured and smoked country ham will last just about forever, but it will continue to get drier and saltier. You can clean and freeze the ham for a tastier result. For the best appearance for the ham, remove any mold growth by rubbing it with a cloth dampened with vinegar. Then wash with cold water. Lightly coat the entire ham with vegetable oil and dust with some paprika for additional color.

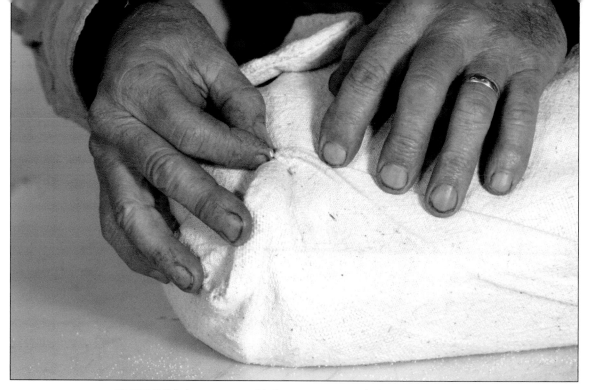

ABOVE: Pull the bottom corners of the bag snug up against the ham and fasten with pins.

BELOW: Tie a heavy cord around the end of the muslin bag.

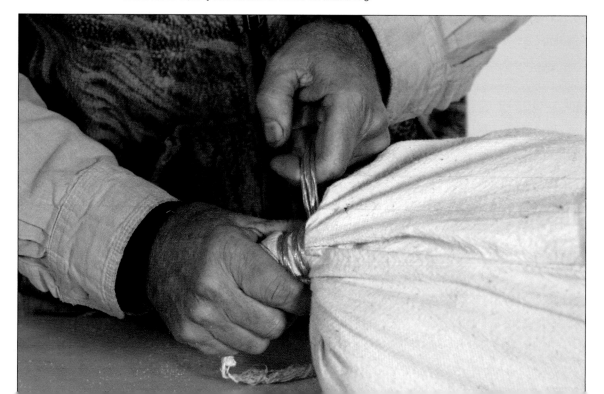

LEFT: Hang the ham in a dry, safe place to age.

Cooking

It takes quite a bit of time to prepare and cure a country ham, and it takes quite a bit of time and effort to properly cook a country ham. Before cooking, wash the ham with cold water; remove any residue salt and cure using a stiff-bristled brush. Place the ham in a large container filled with cold water. Allow to soak overnight or up to 24 hours.

Place the ham in a large container with the skin-side up. Cover with fresh, cold water, and then cover the container with a lid and bring the water to a boil.

BELOW: An aged ham is often cold-smoked for additional flavor and preservation. The aged ham must first be unwrapped and cleaned thoroughly before smoking.

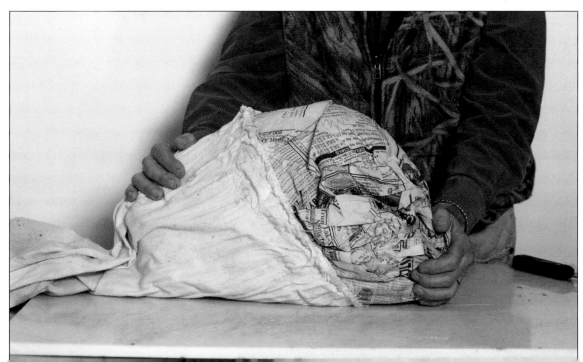

Remove the ham, pour out the water, and repeat the process two to three times. This helps cut down on the salt. Reduce the heat and simmer for 25 minutes per pound, or until the interior temperature reaches 160°F. Remove and allow to drain and cool before carving. Cut away any hardened, dried exterior.

To bake, soak for 24 hours, changing to fresh cold water as frequently as you can, or at least four times. Trim away hardened meat and skin. Place in a large roaster, fat-side up. Pour two to three inches of water in the roasting pan and bake at 325°F until the internal temperature reaches 160°F, about 25 minutes per pound.

Properly cured and aged, a country ham has a salt content of about 4 percent. You can remove some of the salty taste before cooking by slicing to the desired thickness (1/2 inch for fried ham, 1 inch for ham steaks), and then soaking for several hours in cold water. Change the water frequently to remove as much salt as possible.

Breakfast Ham and Redeye Gravy

Trim the fat from the edges and remove any hardened, dried meat. Cut into the edges about one-quarter inch around each ham slice to prevent the edges from curling. Dice a little ham fat and render it in a hot skillet. Add the ham slices, lower the heat to medium, and cook for about 10 minutes, turning frequently to prevent burning. Remove the ham slices and pour in a little water. Stir frequently and simmer for several minutes to deglaze the pan. Serve with the gravy poured over the ham slices. Old-timers served this with homemade biscuits to sop up the tasty gravy.

Home-Curing Bacon

Bacon is actually made of fresh pork bellies, although they are often called "sides." The cut is made by peeling the spareribs away from the side meat, leaving a portion of it as well as the bellies. Then trim the lean meat in the shoulder area so the lean meat over the entire side is approximately the same thickness.

Remove any areas that do not have lean streaks, such as the bellies, and square up the sides. Be sure to cut the sides to fit your curing equipment. Small sides can be cured in a refrigerator. If curing larger sides, or refrigeration space isn't available, place the sides in the cure from late December through early February to cut the risk of spoilage. If the sides have been scalded and scraped with the skins still on, leave the skins on for the curing process. Sides without skin will cure just as well as those with the skin on. Pork bellies must be chilled to about 40°F within 24 to 30 hours of slaughter.

As a kid, I thought our home-cured bacon was quite salty. Over time, I've experimented with different recipes to achieve a milder cure.

A good mild cure recipe consists of

7 pounds canning or pickling salt	3 ounces saltpeter, optional (However, without the saltpeter, the lean meat of the bacon won't have the traditional red color.)
4 pounds light brown sugar	

Apply the cure at the rate of one-half ounce per pound of fresh sides.

In the old days, sides were cured in a cold, dry room, free from pests and the family cat or dog. The sides were covered with a muslin cloth and simply placed on a table that was angled slightly to allow the liquids to drain off.

These days, whether using refrigeration or not, wrapping in food-grade plastic can help deter pests, and is especially helpful when curing in a refrigerator. Weigh the fresh side and prepare the cure. Place the fresh side, skin-side up, on a clean, smooth surface covered with plastic food wrap.

Sprinkle half the cure mixture over the skin side and rub it well into the flesh, coating the edges as well. Turn the side over and sprinkle the remaining cure over the meat side and again coating the ends. Wrap the plastic around the sides and place in a noncorrosive pan or dish. Refrigerate or store in a cold place to cure. If curing outside or

ABOVE: Home-curing bacon is easy and provides a tasty traditional salt-cured meat.

where the sides may freeze during curing, allow the sides to defrost and add one day of curing time for each day they were frozen. Most recipes call for curing the sides 7 days per inch of thickness.

After the bacon has cured for the proper amount of time, remove from the bag, scrub off the salt and cure with lukewarm water, and pat dry with a clean towel. Place back in the refrigerator for a day or two to allow the sides to dry. Cut into 1- to 2-pound packages, then slice to the desired thickness. Wrap and freeze any bacon that won't be consumed within one week. Bacon is also often cold-smoked for flavor.

The Bradley smoker comes with an excellent recipe for home-cured smoked bacon using their Maple Cure. The recipe is for 5 pounds of fresh side or pork belly.

3 tbsp. Bradley Maple Cure (do not use more than this amount for 5 pounds)

I tsp. onion granules or onion powder

I tsp. garlic granules or garlic powder

I tsp. ground white pepper

I to 3 tbsp. maple syrup (optional)

½ to I tsp. imitation maple flavor (optional)

Note: If the meat weighs either more or less than 5 pounds, the amount of cure mix applied must be proportional to that weight.

Weigh the pork. If more than one curing container is used, separately calculate the total weight of the meat that will be placed in each container. Refrigerate the meat while the cure mix is being prepared. Any plastic food container with a tight-fitting lid—or a strong plastic bag—can be used as a curing container. Prepare, calculate, and measure the required amount of curing mixture for each container. Mix this curing blend until uniform. Place the meat in the curing container(s). Rub the cure mix on all surfaces evenly. Cover and

BELOW: You can make up your own cure or use a premixed cure such as the Hi Mountain Buckboard cure.

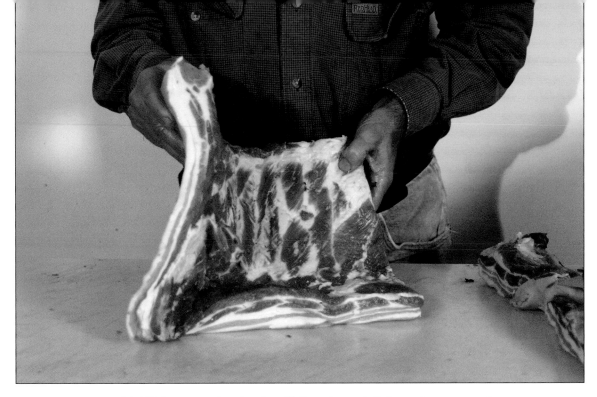

ABOVE: Bacon comes from the side and belly, and excess belly fat must be cut away and the side trimmed up.

BELOW: Regardless of the cure used, the first step is to weigh the side to know how much cure to apply.

ABOVE: Place the side on plastic food wrap and apply the cure.

BELOW: Turn the side over and apply cure to the opposite side.

ABOVE: Wrap the plastic around the side, place in a plastic food container, and place the container in the refrigerator to cure.

refrigerate. The refrigerator temperature should be set between 34°
and 40°F (2.2° to 4.4°C).

Overhaul the pieces of meat after about 12 hours of curing. (*Overhaul* means to rub the surfaces of the meat to redistribute the cure.)
Be sure to wet the meat with any liquid that may have accumulated at
the bottom of the curing container. Overhaul the meat about every
other day until the required curing time has elapsed. Cure one week
per inch: If the thickest piece is one inch, cure one week; if the thickest piece is two inches, cure the whole batch two weeks.

When the curing is finished, rinse each piece of pork very well in
lukewarm water. Drain in a colander and blot with a clean, dry towel.

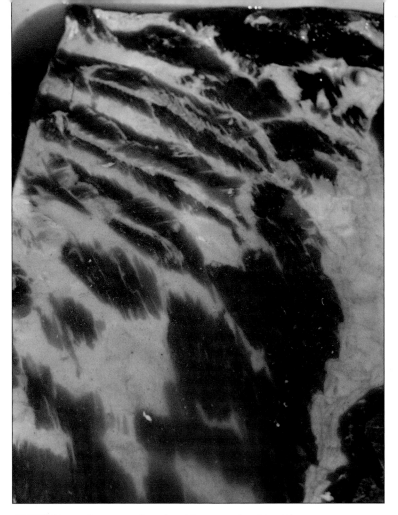

ABOVE: After curing, remove from the refrigerator and soak in cold water.

BELOW: Pat the bacon dry with paper towels, then place it back in the refrigerator a day or two so the salt can equalize.

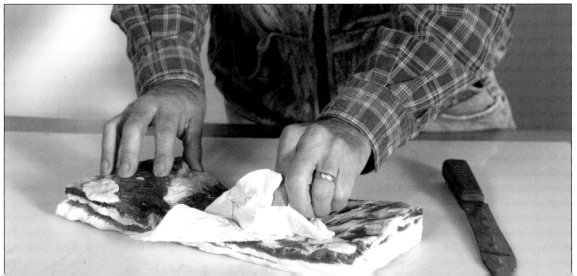

ABOVE: For added flavor, the bacon can be cold-smoked.

Wrap each piece in a paper towel, and then wrap again with newspaper and refrigerate overnight.

The next morning, remove the paper and dry the surface of the meat in front of an electric fan or inside a smoker heated to about 140°F (60°C). If you're using a smoker, make sure the damper is fully open. Do not use smoke when drying. Drying the surface will require 1 to 2 hours.

When the surface is dry, cold-smoke the sides for three hours. If the smoke chamber temperature is higher than 85°F, shorten the smoking time to prevent excessive drying. Raise the smoke chamber temperature to about 150°F. Smoke for two or three hours more or until the surface of the bacon takes on an attractive reddish brown color. Remove the meat and let it cool at room temperature for about one hour. After cooling, place the hunks of bacon in a container—uncovered—and chill overnight. The bacon may be sliced the following morning. Bacon that will not be consumed within about a week should be frozen. The bacon must be cooked before consumption.

Note: If the salt taste is too mild, the next time you make this product, add about 1 teaspoon of cooking or canning salt to the ingredients (do not add more cure). If the salt taste is too strong, reduce the amount of Bradley cure by about 1 teaspoon. This is uncooked meat, and therefore must be cooked before consumption.

Morton Salt Sugar-Cured Bacon

We've been using Morton Salt Sugar Cure (Plain) mix for curing bacon for a long time. It's easy and consistent, and instructions are written on the package. You'll need ½ ounce Sugar Cure mix per pound of meat. Place meat on a piece of food plastic large enough to cover both sides. Sprinkle and rub the skin side thoroughly with half the mix, covering the edges of the meat as well. Turn the meat over and place it and the plastic wrap in a plastic food container or in a noncorrosive tray.

Sprinkle the remainder of the cure over the muscle side of the meat. Rub well to distribute and wrap tightly with the plastic wrap. Place in a refrigerator at 36° to 40°F. Allow to cure for 7 days per inch of thickness. Most sides will be from 1 ½ to 1 ¾ inches thick. On the

BELOW: An electric smoker does a great job of cold-smoking bacon.

fifth day, turn the meat over. At the end of the process, remove the cure, wash the meat in clean, cold water, and place it in the refrigerator for 2 days to equalize. Remove, cut, slice, and freeze.

Hi Mountain Buckboard Bacon Cure

If you don't butcher your own pig, you can sometimes purchase whole pork sides or bellies from a butcher house or your grocery store meat market to make bacon. If you want to try your hand at making bacon but can't find the bellies, Hi Mountain Seasonings suggest using their Buckboard Bacon Cure on a Boston butt pork roast, which is readily available at most supermarkets. This produces an extremely meaty and tasty bacon. You'll need a 4- to 6-pound roast.

First step is to debone and trim the roast. Lay it on a clean cutting surface with the shoulder blade bone to the right. Using a sharp boning knife, remove the shoulder blade bone, keeping the knife as close to the bone as possible. The shoulder blade bone is flat on one side, thus easy to bone out. The opposite side, next to the skin, has a ridge running through the center of it. It takes a bit of patience to cut around this ridge.

With the bone removed, turn the roast fat-side up and trim off any scraps left from boning. Remove the excess fat from the meat. The

BELOW: Before slicing and freezing, trim the bacon to sizes that will fit your slicer.

ABOVE: Slice and freeze the bacon. The end pieces can be packed as "scrap bacon" and used for dicing and cooking. Vacuum packing helps bacon keep fresher longer in the freezer.

best curing thickness is from 3 to 3 ½ inches. Any excess thickness should be trimmed off the back.

Use 16 ounces of Hi Mountain's Buckboard Bacon Cure for each 25 pounds of meat (1 tablespoon plus 1 ¼ teaspoons per pound). Apply the cure to all surfaces of the meat.

Apply the cure to the meat and massage thoroughly, paying particular attention to the sides and ends, and don't forget the cavity left by boning. Leave excess cure on the meaty side of the roast. Place prepared meat in a nonmetallic container. Cover the container with plastic wrap and place in the refrigerator. The proper temperature is 40°F to 45°F. Let the meat stand in the refrigerator at least 10 days, turning on the fifth day.

After curing, remove the meat from the pan, discard any accumulated liquid, and soak in clean, cool water for 1 to 2 hours. Drain and rinse with fresh water, making sure excess cure is removed (rinse cavity thoroughly). Pat dry and let stand at room temperature at least 1 hour. Shape meat, tucking in the edges. Place on a smoking screen or grill. Insert an internal meat thermometer and place meat in a smoker. Heat smoker to 150 degrees for 45 minutes without any smoke. Increase temperature to 200 degrees and start the smoke. Smoke until the internal temperature of the meat reaches 140 degrees. Turn off heat and leave bacon in smoker for 1 hour to cool down.

All smokehouses are different. These differences play an important role in the smoking and the final flavor. Hi Mountain encourages you to explore the capabilities of your smoker by adjusting times, temperatures, and different smoking chips. In some cases, you may want to use the smoker for flavor only, while achieving the necessary heat by conventional means (kitchen oven).

To cook the Hi Mountain Buckboard Cure bacon, slice thin. Buckboard will cook twice as fast as regular bacon, so be careful not to overcook. Try cutting a thicker slice and enjoy a bacon steak.

Sausage

Fresh sausage is a very common salt-cured pork product, and homemade fresh sausage is hard to beat. The first "test batch" of fresh sausage from butchering days is still one of my favorites. Following is the recipe used by our family for several generations.

Burch Family Fresh Pork Sausage

10 lb. pork trimmings from butchering	⅛ cup ground black pepper
¼ cup coarse or canning salt	½ to 1 tbsp. crushed red pepper, or to taste

We keep this basic sausage mix fairly lean, without adding fat, and use only basic salt and pepper flavorings, but it does have a bit of a kick. You can also add a bit of ground cayenne pepper instead of, or in addition to, the crushed red pepper. We grow our own cayenne peppers just for this recipe. This sausage has a really rich, meaty taste and is equally good for breakfast or as a sausage burger.

Spread the cut chunks of meat out on a work surface and sprinkle with salt and peppers. Run the seasoned meat through a grinder using a ⅛-inch plate. In the past, we stuffed the sausage into muslin casings and froze it for future use. To use, simply slice the muslin

BELOW: Salt, along with other flavorings, is used to cure and flavor sausage.

casings into ½-inch-thick patties. We've also simply made the meat into patties and frozen them with wax paper between each patty. The sausage can be stuffed into sheep casings for breakfast links and can also be cold-smoked for more flavor.

More smoked and fresh sausage recipes are available in *The Complete Guide to Sausage Making* by Monte Burch.

Canadian Bacon

Canadian bacon is considered a delicacy by many, but you can easily make it yourself at home. It is made from boneless pork loins, and these are readily available at supermarkets. To start, trim all fat from the loin. If the sinew membrane is still in place, remove it by using a sharp boning knife to fillet it away from the meat. Morton Salt has a good recipe for Canadian bacon.

I boneless pork loin	I tsp. sugar per pound of loin
I tbsp. Morton Tender Quick or Morton Sugar Cure (Plain) mix per pound of loin	

Mix the cure and sugar together thoroughly and rub onto all surfaces of the loin. Place the loin in a food-grade plastic bag and close. Place on a flat pan and in the refrigerator for 3 to 5 days. Remove, soak the loin in cool water for 30 minutes, and brush off any excess cure. Remove from the water and pat dry. Refrigerate uncovered to dry slightly before cooking.

To cook, cut into ⅛-inch-thick slices. Preheat a skillet and brush it with cooking oil. Fry bacon over low heat, turning to brown evenly. It takes about 8 to 10 minutes.

A Canada style, and also one popular in Ireland, is peameal bacon. After curing and drying the loins, coat the outside with a mixture of cornmeal and black and red pepper to taste. Cover with plastic wrap and refrigerate. Slice and sprinkle slices with more cornmeal before frying.

ABOVE: You can also cure pork loins to make your own Canadian bacon.

You can also smoke-cook the cured loin to 165°F in a smoker to create a brown-and-serve-style Canadian bacon.

BELOW: Weigh the loins.

ABOVE: A dry cure is applied and the loins placed in a plastic food bag or plastic wrap, then in a food container and cured in the refrigerator.

BELOW: After curing, wash the excess cure from the bacon and slice. Lightly fry to serve, or freeze for use later.

ABOVE: A form of Canadian bacon, peameal bacon is made by coating the Canadian bacon with pepper and cornmeal and then frying it.

Pickled Pigs Feet

The old-timers used every part and parcel of the hog. "Everything but the squeal," were the words Grandmother Burch used to say. Pickled pigs feet or hocks are an old-time food that is a "delicacy" to many. First step is to clean the feet thoroughly, removing the toes and dewclaws. All the dirt and hair must be removed, as well as the glands between the toes. Cure in a pickle cure of two pounds of Morton Salt Tender Quick per gallon of water. Leave the feet in the cure for 7 to 10 days. Make sure the feet are properly chilled at all times. Remove and wash thoroughly. Place the feet in a pan of hot water and simmer slowly until tender. Cook slowly so the skin doesn't split and pull the feet out of shape.

Chill the feet, and then pack them into a jar and cover with hot spiced vinegar. Here's a good recipe:

4 cleaned, cured, and cooked pigs feet	1 tsp. mustard seed
1 tsp. cayenne pepper	1 tsp. coriander seed
1 tsp. onion powder	¼ tsp. cloves
2 bay leaves	Vinegar to cover
1 tsp. black peppercorns	

Place the feet in a glass jar or crock. Boil the vinegar and spices and pour over the feet. Refrigerate one week. Once opened, the jar must be refrigerated.

BELOW: Pickled pigs feet are made from the feet and hock portions of the leg.

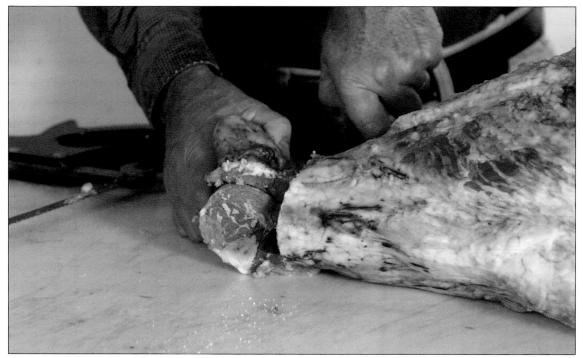

You can also simply cover the pig's feet with cold water, add 2 tablespoons of salt to the recipe, and simmer the feet. Boil the vinegar brine, pour over the cooked feet, and refrigerate.

TRADITIONALLY, FEW CUTS of beef were salt-cured or smoked. This was partly due to the cost of producing beef, and because beef tends to be a drier meat. Almost any beef cut can, however, be cured, and even smoked. The most common cuts to cure are the brisket or a rolled plate. Corned beef and pastrami are traditional favorites and beef jerky or salted and dried beef was a staple for many early Americans in the West. Summer sausage is also a popular cured beef product. Cured beef tongue is considered a delicacy. Veal or a beef calf doesn't do as well cured or dried because it doesn't contain as much fat. Following are some traditional beef recipes.

⑥ Beef

Corned Beef

One of the most popular and common cured beef products is corned beef. This is typically made from the brisket, a tougher meat cut that is also often slow smoke-cooked without curing. Other beef cuts can also be corned, including the rolled plate, chuck, or shoulder. Trim as much fat as possible from the meat and then debone. Beef can be cured using either the immersion or dry-rub method. A number of recipes are available for corning beef, but the following are traditional.

Traditional Corned Beef

25 lb. of beef	2 cups sugar
3 lb. pickling or canning salt	1 tbsp. baking soda

This old-time method was often used with trimmings and smaller cuts of beef from slaughter and was common in the days before refrigeration. The beef was left in the pickle until used, if used within a reasonable time. The cured meat was also sometimes pressure-canned, or even air-dried, as jerky. Note: This recipe does not include nitrites or nitrates, and the meat will not be the traditional red color.

Spread a layer of pickling or canning salt over the bottom of a crock or barrel. Rub pieces of meat well with the salt and make a single layer of meat in the bottom. Sprinkle more salt over the layer and continue to layer with salted meat pieces and salt. Allow the salted meat to stand for 24 hours, then cover with a solution made of 2 cups sugar and 1 tablespoon of baking soda per gallon of water. Place a plate with a heavy object on top to hold the meat submerged in the solution. Leave meat for 4 to 6 weeks at 38°F. Make sure to check the meat frequently. If the brine becomes ropey—which may happen if the temperature rises above 38°F—remove the meat, wash thoroughly in warm water, and repack meat in a clean new container, or in the cleaned original container. Cover with a new brine. At the end of the brining time, remove the meat, wash, and pressure-can, cook, or freeze. The meat must be cooked before consumption.

Morton Salt Corned Beef

Another traditional corned beef recipe utilizes a curing pickle of Morton Salt Tender Quick. First step is to make a pickle brine of two pounds of Morton Salt Tender Quick to each gallon of water. Boil the water first, then stir the cure into the water until it dissolves. Allow the brine to chill before using.

Pack the meat pieces into a clean crock or other nonmetallic container. Pour in the Morton Salt Tender Quick curing pickle until it covers the meat and the chunks begin to float. Place a clean plate on the meat and a weight on top to hold the plate down in the pickle cure.

Cure the meat 5 to 6 days; then overhaul, or pour off the pickle, and repack the meat. Take out all the meat pieces and rearrange them so the top pieces are on the bottom and the bottom pieces are on the top. Weight the meat back down and pour the pickle solution back over it. The meat should cure in the pickle for about 2 days per pound of individual pieces. For instance, pieces that weigh 6 pounds should cure for 12 days. Smaller, 4-pound pieces will cure in 8 days. After curing, remove the pieces, wash in warm water, and pressure-can, cook to use immediately, or freeze.

Easy-Does-It Pickle Cure Corned Beef

You can also create a corned beef quite easily in your refrigerator using a 3- to 5-pound beef brisket purchased at your local supermarket. The brisket should be of good quality and well trimmed with no excess fat. Large briskets should be cut in half for easier storing and curing. The brisket is cured using a pickle cure.

BELOW: Corned beef is a traditional and popular salt-cured meat. And corning beef is quite easy to do.

ABOVE: A trimmed beef brisket is the common cut used for making corned beef as well as pastrami.

BELOW: The brisket is cut into two pieces for easy processing, weighed, and a cure is applied by hand.

ABOVE: The cure-treated brisket is placed in a plastic food bag and cured in the refrigerator.

2 cups Morton Salt Tender Quick	2 tsp. black peppercorns
1 cup brown sugar	1 tsp. mustard seeds
3 quarts water	1 tsp. whole cloves

Boil the water, then reduce to a simmer and stir in the Tender Quick and spices. Allow the brine to cool completely. Place the brisket pieces in a nonmetallic container and cover with the pickle cure. Weight the briskets down. Or place the briskets in large food-container bags, add the pickle, and seal well. In this case, place the bagged briskets into a tray. Each day turn the briskets in their pickle mix. Curing time is 7 to 10 days.

After curing, wash and pressure-can, cook, or freeze.

Deli-Style Corned Beef

The Morton Salt folks also have an even easier, dry-rub method of preparing corned beef.

ABOVE: Remove the beef from the refrigerator and wash off any remaining cure.

4–6 lb. beef brisket	I tsp. ground paprika
5 tbsp. Morton Tender Quick or Morton Sugar Cure (Plain) mix	I tsp. ground bay leaves
	I tsp. ground allspice
2 tbsp. brown sugar	½ tsp. garlic powder
I tbsp. ground black pepper	

Trim the surface of fat from the brisket. In a small bowl, mix Morton Tender Quick mix or Morton Sugar Cure (Plain) mix, sugar, and spices. Rub the mixture into all sides of the brisket. Place the brisket in a food-grade plastic bag and close the end securely. Refrigerate and cure 5 days per inch of meat thickness at the thickest portion of the brisket.

Place brisket in a Dutch oven or a large pot. Add water to cover. Bring to a boil, reduce heat, and simmer until tender.

ABOVE: Simmer in fresh water, cool, and then thin slice for serving.

Pastrami

Corned beef is cooked by simmering; pastrami is a beef deli meat that is also flavored by smoke cooking. It also has a spice crust added. The first step is to create the corned beef as above. Again, make sure you use a quality cut of beef brisket.

After the brisket has been corned, rinse in cool water and scrub off any excess cure. Completely submerge the meat in clean, cool water and hold it down with a plate. Leave for about an hour to help remove remaining exterior cure. Make up the following spice crust mix:

¼ cup cracked black peppercorns	I tsp. crushed red pepper
¼ cup crushed coriander	I tsp. garlic powder
I tbsp. crushed mustard seed	I tsp. onion powder

Mix the spice ingredients in a small bowl. Place corned brisket fat-side up on a large piece of plastic food wrap. Apply the crust mix to

the brisket and rub over the meat surface and onto the ends and sides as well. Press the ingredients into the meat surface as much as possible. Turn the brisket over and repeat for the opposite side. Wrap the plastic food wrap tightly around the meat and place on a tray. Place in the refrigerator for 24 hours.

ABOVE: Then the pastrami crust of spices are added.

BELOW: The spiced brisket is placed in a plastic food bag and in the refrigerator for 24 hours.

ABOVE: The meat is removed from the refrigerator and patted dry, then smoked in a smoker until the internal temperature is 160°F. Chill and then thin-slice.

Remove the meat from the refrigerator and pat dry. Place on a smoking tray or screen and place in your smoker. You can also make a small hole in one corner and hang the brisket in the smoker using a smoker hook. Smoke for about an hour at 225°F. Remove and wrap tightly with aluminum foil. Smoke-cook for 2 to 3 hours more or until the internal temperature reaches 160°F. Remove and steam until the meat is tender.

Bradley Smoker Pastrami

You can create a true deli-style smoked pastrami using this recipe from Bradley Smoker. The company suggests using the recipe with either beef or wild game. The recipe utilizes Bradley Sugar Cure mix and is for 5 pounds of meat. Exceedingly fat meat, or exceedingly lean meat, such as beef round, should be avoided.

5 lb. beef or wild game	I tsp. oregano
3 tbsp. Bradley Sugar Cure (Do not use more than this amount for 5 pounds.)	I tsp. paprika
	½ tsp. allspice
2 tsp. garlic powder	½ tsp. powdered ginger
2 tsp. onion powder	Light corn syrup and coarsely ground black pepper
I tsp. red pepper	
I tsp. white pepper	

Note: If the meat weighs more or less than 5 pounds, the amount of cure mix must be proportional to that weight.

Pastrami is thoroughly cooked. It may be steamed, hot-smoked, boiled, or oven-roasted. A modified form of hot water cooking is one of the methods suggested here, but other methods may be employed. Hot smoking or oven roasting can cause excessive drying.

Cut off loose flesh and remove bloody spots and gristle. Remove excess fat. Cut the meat into pieces, the sizes you want to process. The thicker meat requires longer curing time. Rinse all pieces in cold water and drain them in a colander. Blot dry with a paper towel. Measure the thickest chunk of meat and allow 6 days' curing time for every inch of meat. Weigh the meat. If more than one curing container will be used, calculate separately the total weight of the meat that will be placed in each container. Prepare, calculate, and measure the required amount of curing mixture for each container. Evenly rub the cure mix on all meat surfaces. Place the meat in the curing containers. Cover and refrigerate. The refrigerator temperature should be set between 34°F and 40°F. Overhaul the pieces of meat after about 12 hours of curing. Wet the meat with any liquid that may have accumulated at the bottom of the curing container. Overhaul the meat every other day until the required curing time has elapsed. After the curing, rinse each piece of meat in lukewarm water. Drain in a colander and blot with paper towels. Using a basting brush, "paint" each piece of pastrami with light corn syrup or honey diluted with a little water. (This will help the pepper stick to the meat.) Wait a few minutes to allow the surface to become tacky.

Sprinkle and press on coarsely ground pepper. Wrap each piece of beef in a paper towel, and then wrap in newspaper. Refrigerate overnight.

Remove the newspaper and the paper towel and hang the pieces in the smoke chamber, or place on smoking racks. Dry at about 140°F until the surface is dry (about an hour). Do not use smoke during the drying period. To avoid excessive drying and excessively dark coloration, smoke at less than 85 degrees if possible. Smoke the pastrami for 3 to 6 hours, depending on how smoky you want the meat. Raise the temperature to about 145°F for an hour or two toward the end of the smoking time if a darker coloration is desired.

Begin heating water in a large soup pot. Raise the water temperature to 200°F. While the water is heating, wrap each piece of pastrami in plastic food wrap and place in a plastic food cooking bag. Expel as much air as possible from the bag before tying or sealing it. Bag all the meat pieces and put in the hot water cooker at one time. Press and weight them down below the water surface. Maintain the hot water temperature at 200°F and cook the meat about 2 ½ hours. This long period of cooking will make the meat tender—even gristle will be tender. A thermometer is not required because the cooking time and rather high temperature will ensure the meat is fully cooked. Caution: Raising the water temperature to the boiling point will cause the plastic bags to balloon, the water to overflow the pot, and the meat to shrink excessively. Know that you can maintain the proper water temperature before immersing the bagged meat. If you find it impossible to maintain the correct temperature, simply place the meat pieces in simmering water and slowly simmer until the desired internal temperature is reached.

Remove the meat from the hot water. Carefully open the plastic bags, remove the plastic wrapping, and drain the meat in a colander. Cool at room temperature for about 2 hours and then refrigerate uncovered, overnight. The next morning the pastrami should be sliced, wrapped, and frozen. Freeze the portions that will not be consumed in one week.

Instead of cooking the pastrami in hot water, it can also be roasted in an oven, or steamed. In either case, the pastrami is done when the internal temperature is 170°F. An aluminum foil tent or oven cooking bag should be used if the pastrami is cooked in an oven. If it is steamed, wrap each piece in plastic food wrap before steaming, and use an electronic meat thermometer with a cable probe to monitor the internal temperature. A steamer may be improvised by using a large pan with an elevated rack inside. Cover with a lid.

Corned Tongue

Corned beef tongue was a delicacy in the old days, and it can still provide an unusual delicacy. Actually, both beef and pork tongues were corned, although pork tongues were more often added to sausage or headcheese products, rather than cured. The old-time recipe shown is for a 3- to 4-pound tongue and calls for saltpeter or potassium or sodium nitrate and pickling salt, although you can substitute any commercial curing mix.

1 cup pickling salt	¼ tsp. ground cloves
½ teaspoon saltpeter	4 bay leaves
8 cups water	¼ cup finely minced onion
2 tbsp. brown sugar	2 cloves garlic, finely minced
1 tbsp. mixed pickling spices	1 medium onion, sliced
1 tsp. paprika	1 tsp. whole black peppercorns
½ tsp. freshly ground black pepper	

Create a brine cure by dissolving the salt in the water in a large saucepan. Add in the spices. Boil for 5 minutes and then cool. Place the tongue in a crock or nonmetallic container. Sprinkle the minced garlic and onion over the tongue. Pour the brine solution over the tongue and weight it down with a plate to make sure it is covered and submerged. A water-filled jar can be placed on the plate to keep it down. Place in a refrigerator and allow to cure for 3 weeks at 38°F.

Remove and turn the tongue once a week. Remove the cured tongue, rinse off the brine, and place in a large kettle or Dutch oven. Cover with hot water and add the bay leaves, whole peppers, and sliced onion. Cover and simmer for 3 to 4 hours (1 hour per pound) or until tender. Remove the tongue and cool. Slit the skin on the underside from the large end to the tip and peel it off. Slice diagonally and chill. Serve cold.

Beef Summer Sausage

Beef was, and still is, salt-cured, and often smoked, to create summer sausage, a delicious snack food. In most instances, pork is added to the mix. This is a great use of trimmings from both beef and pork. One method is to grind the meats and freeze in 1-pound bags. Take out of the freezer, thaw, and make the amount of summer sausage desired. Any number of recipes is available for the various

types of summer sausage. For more recipes, see *The Complete Guide to Sausage Making* by Monte Burch.

3 lb. beef trimmings	¼ tsp. ground red pepper
2 lb. pork trimmings	I tsp. garlic powder
5 tbsp. curing salt	I tsp. onion powder
½ tsp. ground black pepper	I cup cold water

Weigh the meats and grind using a 3/16-inch plate. Mix spices and salt and pour over the ground meat. Blend thoroughly. Place in a covered plastic or glass bowl and refrigerate overnight. Roll into logs 1 ½ x 12 inches long, wrap in plastic or foil or stuff in 2 ½-inch fibrous casings, and refrigerate overnight again. Cook on oven racks at 325°F, or smoke at 130°F for two hours. Raise temperature to 160 degrees and smoke for 2 more hours. Raise the temperature to 180 degrees and cook until the internal temperature reaches 160 degrees.

LEFT: One of the most popular salt-cured beef products is summer sausage, and it's quick and easy to make.

Beef jerky is another very common and easy-to-make salt-cured beef. The traditional jerky is made by thin-slicing the meat, soaking it in a salt-and-spice mixture, and then drying.

Beef Jerky

A very common use of beef, especially in the West, was to dry it into jerky. This extremely handy food could be carried in saddlebags for a quick meal. These days beef jerky is still a very popular snack food. You can easily make your own beef jerky using the following recipe, which I've been using for almost forty years.

2 lb. lean beef (round), thinly sliced	I tsp. black pepper
I cup of soy sauce	Ground red pepper, to suit
I tbsp. garlic powder	Water to cover
I tbsp. onion powder	

Although many recipes contain salt as a curing agent, other ingredients can be used to replace the salt. Soy sauce is substituted for the salt in this recipe. Mix the ingredients and place with the meat in a glass bowl, plastic container, or sealable plastic bag and refrigerate for 12 hours or overnight. Remove, drain, and pat dry. Dry in an oven or dehydrator until the meat bends but does not break. To dry in the oven, set on cookie cooling racks over cookie pans, set oven at lowest temperature, and crack door open. For more information on making your own jerky, read *The Complete Jerky Book* by Monte Burch.

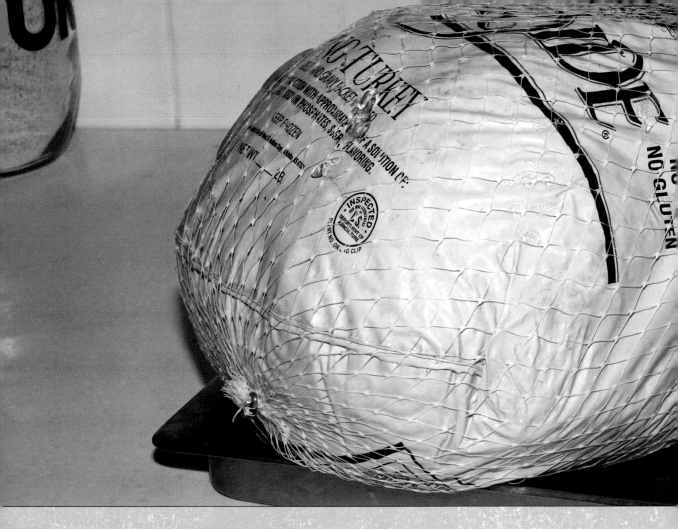

ALTHOUGH NOT AS commonly salt-cured and smoked as some other meats, poultry treated in this manner can be extremely delicious. Curing and smoking provides an unusual way to prepare these common and economical meats. Poultry may be smoked, then cooked, cured, and smoke-cooked, or simply smoke-cooked. Poultry may also be processed in salt brine, to which liquid smoke flavoring has been added, and cooked in the oven. This alleviates the smoking process for those without a way of smoking. In all cases, however, poultry must be hot-smoked or smoke-cooked rather than cold-smoked as with some other meats. With poultry, the smoking is for flavor rather than preservation. Poultry that has been cured and smoke-cooked has a unique flavor, has the pink color of smoked foods, and has a slightly increased refrigerator storage life. Cured and smoked poultry can be

7 Poultry

stored in the refrigerator for up to 2 weeks. Poultry that has not been cured but merely smoke-cooked, however, must be treated and stored just like other cooked poultry. Cured and smoked poultry, like other meats such as ham, can be served hot or cold. The meat also makes delicious sandwiches and salads as well as party snacks.

As with other meats, it's extremely important to start out with quality meat, and that is especially so with poultry, as the meat quickly turns rancid. If the birds are freshly slaughtered, they must be well chilled before curing. All poultry must be chilled to below 40°F immediately after slaughter. Once chilled, the birds must be cured within 2 to 3 days. Purchased processed birds may also be cured and smoked.

ABOVE: Poultry can also be brine-cured and smoked.

In most instances, poultry is brine-cured. This may be by immersion, in the case of smaller poultry, or with the addition of pump curing for turkeys and larger poultry. As it is not a preservative, the salt-brine cure used for poultry is generally milder than for other meats in order to enhance and bring out the natural flavor of the meat.

Like other meats, poultry can be cured using a homemade curing mix or commercially prepared cures. A variety of spices can be used for added seasoning. Some commercial cures also have spices added to the cure, or in separate packets to be added to the cure. Sodium nitrite is usually added to the commercial cures, but can also be added to your own mix. Nitrite provides a light pink coloring after the meat has been cured and heated. Poultry meat that has been smoked without the addition of the nitrite will have more of a tannish white color.

General Brining and Curing Techniques

A number of different curing formulas can be used. If you want to make up your own brine, a basic brine consists of 2 pounds of non-iodized canning or pickling salt, 1 pound of brown sugar, and 3 gallons of water. One tablespoon of liquid smoke can be added if you are unable to smoke the bird but want the smoked flavor.

If you want to use brine with sodium nitrite or saltpeter, add 1.6 ounces of saltpeter to each gallon of water needed to cover the meat. In addition to the basic brine ingredients, seasonings may be added, including black pepper, bay leaves, garlic, basil, oregano, lemon pepper, and thyme.

Use cold water, 36°F to 40°F, to make up the brine. Add ice to cold water to create the volume of chilled water needed to cover the poul-

BELOW: Poultry is salt-cured only for flavor, and a mild cure is used. You can make up your own, or use a prepared cure.

try. Add the ingredients, stirring until the solution is clear. Immediately apply the brine to the poultry. Use plastic or noncorrosive containers to hold the brine and poultry. Any poultry can be brined and smoked—whole poultry, boned parts, or parts such as drumsticks and wings. Place the chilled meat in the container, then pour the chilled brine over the meat. Place a plate and a weight over the meat to make sure it is completely submerged. A zippered plastic food bag filled with water and securely closed can also be used as a weight. Make sure the brine goes into the body cavity of whole birds.

In general, the brine will soak into the meat at approximately ½ inch per 24 hours at 34°F to 38°F. Small broilers, of 2 pounds or less, as well as small birds such as quail and Cornish hens should be kept in the brine 2 to 3 days. For larger birds, keep in the cure 1 day per pound. Every 3 days, remove the birds from the containers, stir up the brine, and repack the carcasses or pieces back in the brine, shifting the piece around to more evenly distribute the brine.

BELOW: A pickle-cure brine is made up, the poultry submerged in the pickle, and then placed in the refrigerator to cure.

A common brine for large quantities is as follows:

5 lb. noniodized salt	1⅛ lb. cure (containing 6.25 percent sodium nitrite)
3 lb. brown sugar	5 gallons of water

Pack birds into a plastic food-safe or glass container and measure the amount of water needed to cover the birds. Adjust the recipe to suit the amount of water needed to use as cover. Dissolve the salt, sugar, and cure in a portion of the water and then add the rest of the water. A general time to brine a bird is 1 day per pound of individual birds.

A brine for nonsmoked but smoke-flavored chicken is as follows:

1 cup non-iodized, canning or pickling salt	1 tsp. oregano
¾ cup brown sugar	1 tsp. thyme
1 tsp. ground garlic	1 tsp. liquid smoke
1 tsp. dried basil	1 gallon cold water

Soak the poultry in the brine for 24 hours, or 1 day per pound, and then roast in the oven.

Following is a good homemade chicken brine that requires only common pantry items and oven roasting.

3 lemons	5 jalapeño peppers, split and seeded
1 cup canning or pickling salt	1 tbsp. dried basil
¾ cup brown sugar	1 tbsp. dried oregano
¼ cup crushed and diced garlic	1 tbsp. dried thyme
3 bay leaves, crushed	1 gallon cold water
¼ cup whole black peppercorns	

Zest and juice the lemons. Dissolve the salt, sugar, and spices in the water and juice. Brine small fryer chickens for 24 hours, larger birds for 1 day per pound. Keep refrigerated at all times. Rinse, pat dry, and oven-roast.

Injection Brining

Larger birds, such as turkeys, should be cured by the addition of pump, stitch, or injection curing. Otherwise, it takes too long for the cure to work, and results are not as consistent. Weigh the bird and make note of the weight. Stitch-pump the brine into the thickest areas of the breast and thighs, using a large syringe with a no. 12 needle or a meat injector. Make sure you pump the brine into all the muscle areas as well as the joints. To avoid lots of injection holes in the skin, try to use only a few holes for several injections, moving the needle around under the skin as necessary. The carcass should be injected with brine of about 10 to 11 percent of the bird's weight, or until the bird weighs 11 percent more than before injection. Then submerge

BELOW: Larger birds, such as turkeys, should be injection-brined as well.

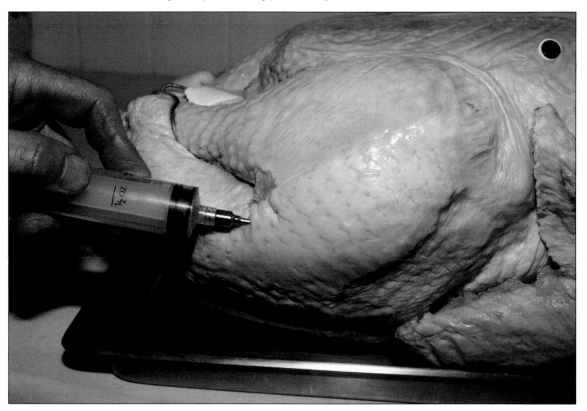

ABOVE: poultry is rinsed with cold water to remove the brine.

the carcass into the remaining brine for 2 to 3 days. Make sure the bird is weighted down and kept submerged in the brine. Remove from the brine and wash in cold tap water, allow to soak for an hour or so, changing the water and rewashing frequently. Remove from the water and allow the carcass to dry for about a half hour before cooking.

Smoking and Cooking

A simple method of cooking is to brush liquid smoke over the carcass and then oven-roast at 300°F to 325°F. Cook to an internal temperature of 165°F. Keep covered to retain moisture.

ABOVE: Cured and smoked poultry must be hot-smoked or cooked to an internal temperature of 165°F. A smoked-only turkey must be cooked to an internal temperature of 175°F.

For a true smoke-flavor bird, use the hot-smoke or cook/smoke method with a smoker. Allow the carcass to air-dry thoroughly and place in a stockinette or cheesecloth in order to suspend the bird, or place on the smoker rack. Smoke at 140°F with a very dense smoke for 4 hours. It's also important to maintain a high humidity to prevent the meat from drying excessively. Use dampened wood chips or place a pan of water or marinade over the heat source. Add water as it evaporates. If suspended in the smokehouse, hang tail-end up. After 4 hours, raise the smoker temperature gradually to 190°F to 200°F. After the first 4 hours, the exterior of the carcass should have a nice browned look. To prevent the meat from further drying out, wrap the carcass in aluminum foil. Cook at 190°F to 200°F until the internal temperature of the meat reaches 165 degrees for a cured/smoked turkey, 175°F for a smoke-cooked turkey.

Use a meat thermometer, inserted into the thickest part of the breast, to determine the internal temperature. It will normally take from 12 to 16 hours total to smoke-cook a turkey. You can shorten the time by smoking 4 to 6 hours, or until the outside reaches a nice rich brown color, and then place in a roaster and cook at 300 to 325 degrees in an oven until the internal temperature reaches 165°F for a cured bird and 175°F for a smoke-cooked bird. Cover with foil during oven cooking to prevent the skin from drying out.

Smoke-cooked turkey is extremely perishable and should be treated the same as fresh cooked turkey. Cure-smoked turkey or poultry must be refrigerated, or may be freezer-stored for as long as one year. Use a moisture/vapor-proof bag for storage.

Recipes

Easy-Does-It, Noncured, Smoked Turkey

Bradley Smoker offers some excellent easy-does-it turkey cooking tips with their electric smokers. The Bradley smoker comes with a cold-smoke attachment, and you can use it to add a true-smoked flavor very easily to regular oven-baked turkey. Place the washed, thawed, and dried turkey into the Bradley smoker and place 3 or 4 bisquettes in the smoke unit. Turn on the smoke unit and allow to smoke for 60 to 80 minutes. Once the turkey is smoked, prepare and cook it in your kitchen oven as you normally would. The flavor is amazingly different.

Smoked/Fried Turkey

If you want to add a totally different and delicious flavor to your oil-fried turkey, try cold-smoking it in your Bradley smoker for 60 to 100 minutes before frying. Place the thawed, washed, and dried bird into the smoker and use the cold-smoke unit. After this smoking period, season and deep-fry the bird per your fryer's instructions. You get a deep-fried bird with a rich smoked flavor.

The following recipes are for brining and then both smoking and cooking a 20- to 26-pound turkey in the Bradley smoker. Brining adds flavor and moisture, providing an incredibly rich-flavored and succulent smoked turkey. Your fried-bird-loving friends will beg to learn how you did it.

Brine-Smoked Big Bird

2 cups Bradley Demerara Cure	1 tsp. dried rosemary
1 cup brown sugar	½ tsp. dried sage
¼ cup molasses	2 bay leaves
2 tbsp. whole peppercorns	1 ½ gallons water
2 tbsp. allspice berries	½ gallon apple cider
1 tbsp. whole cloves	1 ½ cups Jim Beam Bourbon

In a large pot, combine all ingredients and bring to a boil. Then remove the pot and cool to 40°F. Place a clean turkey in a large plastic pail or cooler, breast-side down, and completely cover with the brine. If needed, add more water and apple cider. Place an ice bag on top of the bird to keep it completely submerged, cover the container, and set aside in a refrigerator for 16 hours.

After brining is completed, discard all of the brine solution, dry the bird, and place in a smoker preheated to 205°F to 220°F. You will need to cook the turkey at least 30 minutes per pound or until the internal temperature reaches 165°F. Smoke the bird with Bradley Jim Beam wood bisquettes for about 4 hours at the start of the smoke cooking. It is not recommended to have stuffing in the turkey during the smoke-cooking period.

Brine-Injected Tom Turkey

This recipe is a variation of the previous recipe.

2 cups Bradley Demerara Cure	2 tbsp. minced fresh garlic
2¼ cups kosher salt	3 white onions finely chopped
1½ cups brown sugar	9 tbsp. black peppercorns (ground or cracked)
3 bunches tarragon	
3 bunches fresh parsley	6 lemons (halved and squeezed)
6 bay leaves	

Add all the ingredients to 3 gallons of water, heat, and bring to a boil. Stir until salt and sugar are completely dissolved. Chill the brine down to 40°F. Once chilled and ready to use, remove 3 to 6 cups of solution and strain through a paper coffee filter. Inject this mixture into the bird with a food injector. Then place turkey in the remainder of the brine and cover completely using a bag of ice to weigh the bird down. Place in a refrigerator for 16 to 24 hours. Remove the turkey from the brine and discard the brine. Keep refrigerated 12 to 24 hours before smoke cooking. Place the bird into the 200°F to 220°F preheated Bradley smoker and smoke for about four hours. Then continue cooking for at least 30 minutes per pound or until the internal temperature reaches 150°F. Remove the bird and place it in a conventional oven preheated to 325°F to crisp the skin, and finish cooking to at least 165°F internal temperature.

Cured Roast Chicken

From Morton Salt, this is an easy way to produce a cured and smoke-flavored oven-roasted chicken.

3 lb. broiler-fryer, whole	2 quarts water
I cup Morton Tender Quick or Morton Sugar Cure (Plain) mix	Liquid smoke

In a large bowl, dissolve Morton Tender Quick or Morton Sugar Cure (Plain) mix in water. Wash chicken and place in the brine. Weight down chicken with small ceramic plate or bowl so it is completely covered with brine. If necessary, prepare more brine using the same proportions as above. Refrigerate and allow to cure for 24 hours. Rinse chicken thoroughly in cold water to remove excess salt; pat dry. Refrigerate chicken for 6 to 12 hours before cooking so the salt content will equalize.

Place chicken, breast-side up, on a rack in a shallow roasting pan. Brush the chicken with liquid smoke. Roast at 375°F until meat thermometer registers 180°F, about 1 ¼ to 1 ¾ hours, or until the thigh feels soft when pressed between your fingers.

Whole Smoked Chicken

This Bradley Smoker recipe uses any of the Bradley Cures, including Honey, Maple, and Demerara. The recipe is for 5 pounds of chicken. If the meat weighs either more or less than 5 pounds, the amount of cure mix applied must be proportional to the weight, but do not use more than 3 tablespoons per 5 pounds of chicken. For instance, if the weight of the meat is 2 ½ pounds, then each ingredient, including the Bradley Cure, needs to be cut in half.

The dark meat of the chicken will be pink even when it is fully cooked, and this meat will taste a little like cured ham. You may use any size of bird, or you may mix different sizes of birds. All the birds, regardless of size, may be processed in the same curing container. The sizes are not important because the amount of cure is measured and applied to each bird according to its weight. Use young, tender, well-chilled chickens that are suitable for frying or broiling. Three steps are involved: curing, smoking, and roasting.

5 lb. chicken	1 tsp. sage, rubbed (packed in the spoon)
3 tbsp. Bradley Cure	
2 tsp. poultry seasoning (packed in the spoon)	1 tsp. oregano
	1 tsp. ground white pepper
2 tsp. onion powder	1 tsp. paprika
1 tsp. MSG (optional)	½ tsp. dill weed
1 tsp. garlic powder	½ tsp. crushed bay leaf

Rinse and clean the bird or birds and let drain in a colander. Next, use a sturdy fork to pierce the chicken all over, especially the legs and breast. Prepare the proper amount of cure according to the weight of the bird. (If more than one bird is being cured, prepare the proper amount for each bird.) Apply the cure uniformly to the bird; a shaker with large holes works well for this. Be sure to apply the cure to the inside of the body cavity as well as to the outside skin. Cure the chicken in the refrigerator for at least 4 days. Rub all surfaces to redistribute (overhaul) once a day during that period. The refrigerator temperature should be set between 34°F and 40°F.

At the end of the curing period, rinse the bird inside and out in cool water, and blot it inside and out as well. Stuff the body cavity with paper towels that have been wrapped around crumpled newspapers. Store the bird in the refrigerator overnight, preferably with the tail pointed upward. Put a paper towel and several layers of newspaper under the chicken to absorb the water.

The next morning, set up the smoker to finish drying the chicken. Preheat smoker to about 140°F. If possible, hang the bird in the smoker with the tail pointing up. This allows the melted fat and juices to fall freely into the smoker drip tray instead of collecting in the body cavity. Dry the bird in the smoker at 140°F. After the skin is dry to the touch (about an hour), cold-smoke it for 3 hours at 85°F, or as low a temperature as possible. (The cold-smoke unit is excellent for this.) This will provide a mild smoke flavor. If you like a stronger smoke flavor, smoke the chicken for about 6 hours. Apply cooking oil to the chicken and hot-smoke at 145°F until the bird takes on a beautiful reddish brown color (probably 2 more hours).

Remove the chicken from the smoker. Apply cooking oil to the skin again. Cover well with foil, but do not seal the foil tightly—leave a few openings for steam to escape. (Because the chicken has been browned in the smoker, additional browning is undesirable, and the foil prevents this. The loose wrapping of foil allows some steam to escape, but it also prevents excessive drying). Add about 1 tablespoon of water to the inside of the foil, and roast the bird in a kitchen oven at 350°F for about 2 hours. Use a meat thermometer to test for doneness. When the internal temperature is 180°F, it is done.

Hi Mountain Game Bird and Poultry Brine Mix

Hi Mountain Seasonings has a very-easy-to-use poultry brine mix. Everything needed, including cure and spices, is included. The brine mix comes in two packets; each will make up 1 gallon of brine. Poultry should be well chilled before curing. Dissolve 1 pouch in 1 gallon of ice water (34°F to 38°F) in a nonmetallic container. Immerse the poultry into the brine, completely covering it. Weight down the bird to keep it submerged. Place in a refrigerator for 24 hours.

Preheat the smoker to 140°F. Remove the poultry from the brine and rinse with fresh tap water. Pat dry and place in a smoker without smoke for the first hour to dry the bird. Add smoke and raise the temperature to 200°F. Smoke until desired internal temperature of 175°F is reached. If you cannot get the poultry to the desired internal temperature in the smoker, when the desired color is reached, place the poultry in the kitchen oven to finish. Smoke time will vary depending on the type of smoker, location, outside temperature, and so forth.

BELOW: Prepared brines are easy to use.

⑧
Fish

SALTED, CURED, PICKLED, and smoked fish are age-old foods that are enjoyed worldwide. Fish preserved using these methods have been a staple of many cultures, including the Native Americans. Even today, catches of many saltwater and larger freshwater fish often result in an excess of fish. Although an excess amount of fresh fish can, of course, be frozen, salting, curing, and smoking are traditional methods of preserving excess amounts of fresh fish. The most important use of curing and smoking these days, however, is more for flavor rather than preservation. It's a great way of producing exquisite gourmet meals such as smoked salmon, trout, tuna, halibut, catfish, and inland stripers, even bass and bluegill, in addition to other seafood delicacies. Smoking fish is also fun and interesting. In earlier days, when curing and smoking was primarily for preservation, large amounts of salt were commonly used. These days salt curing and smoking is mostly for adding flavor and for the sake of appearance. These lightly salted and smoked foods are not, however, preserved, and improper cooking or smoking can cause serious, even fatal, food poisoning. Lightly salted and smoked fish must be kept refrigerated at 38°F, or frozen for future consumption.

Salting and Smoking

Three very important steps must be taken in salting and smoking fish. The first is to make sure the fish is cleaned properly and kept well chilled. Second, fish must be brined long enough to make sure there is an adequate amount of salt in the meat. Third, fish can be cold-smoked and then cooked, or smoke-cooked. Cold smoking, or smoking below 80°F to 90°F, is the most complicated, with long smoking times and less consistent results, with more chances for food safety problems. Most smoked fish these days is smoke-cooked. Fish must be heated to 160°F internal temperature, and this temperature must be maintained at least 30 minutes during smoke cooking or smoking and heating.

Although almost any fish can be smoked, fatty fish can be brined and smoked easier than leaner fish because the lean fish absorb the salt quicker, and it's easy to get the fish too salty and smoked too dry. Good freshwater choices include catfish, suckers, inland stripers, white bass, shad, and sturgeon. Trout are also an excellent choice for smoking. Almost all saltwater species, and especially the more oily species—including mackerel, sablefish, and tuna—can be smoked. Even the smaller fish—such as herring and smelt—can be successfully smoked. The salmon species are some of the most popular and common smoked varieties.

Choosing and Preparing Salmon

If curing and smoking your own freshly caught salmon, do so as quickly as possible, keeping the flesh well chilled or frozen until you are ready to smoke. Clean the salmon and eviscerate. Remove the tail, fins, and head. Cut about ½ to 1 inch off the belly on each side. Leave the skin on, or remove as desired. Pull out any pinbones. For small salmon, cut into 3-inch-wide steaks. Then cut the steaks apart along the backbone. For large salmon, cut into 1 ½- to 2-inch-wide pieces.

If purchasing salmon for smoking, it's important to get good-quality, fresh salmon. The flesh should be evenly colored, with no mottling, and clean and solid. Salmon flesh that is mushy is suspect and will not cure and smoke properly. If the head is still on the fish, the eyes should be bright and clear. The skin should have a bright, shiny appearance. Quite often, however, you will be purchasing prepackaged salmon, and it's more difficult to determine quality. If the salmon is fresh, press on the flesh. If it doesn't spring back when you remove your finger, it's probably spoiled, or "old." The different salmon varieties have different qualities. The salmon with higher oil contents have more flavor and result in a more moist smoked food. These include the sockeye, king, and Atlantic salmon. Salmon with lower oil contents and a lighter flavor include the pink and chum. A great deal of the Atlantic salmon is farm-raised and has a fairly firm, oily flesh.

Smoke only top-quality fish, either fresh or frozen. Freezer-burned or dried-out fish from your freezer won't provide good-quality food. Freshly caught fish should be thoroughly cleaned to remove all blood, slime, and harmful bacteria. Either fillet or split the fish. Either skin or leave the skin on depending on species, recipe, and preference. Larger fish can be cut into steaks. Regardless, the pieces should not be more than 1 inch thick, or they may not smoke properly and then could spoil. Cut all pieces into uniform sizes so all will be salted equally and will smoke evenly. Keep fish to be smoked as cool as possible at all times. The ideal temperature is 38°F. Check your refrigerator to make sure it is at or below this temperature. Avoid cross-contamination by not handling raw fish in the same area where smoked fish is wrapped, prepared, or kept.

Parasites such as tapeworms and nematodes can also be a problem in some fish, especially when you're using low-salt, low-temperature, cold-smoke preserving methods. These parasites can survive some salt brining and smoking methods, creating serious health problems. Freezing the raw fish at a temperature of 0°F for two weeks or longer can destroy the parasites. Check your freezer to make sure it reaches the proper temperature. Frozen fish should be thawed in a cool place or placed in cool water to thaw. Do not refreeze. The best method is to first process the fish, cutting into proper sizes, and then freezing.

Hot smoking or smoke cooking, which means raising the internal temperature to at least 160°F, and holding the fish for 30 minutes at this temperature, kills the parasites as well as other bacteria.

Brining

Fish can be salt-cured by either dry cure or brining. Brining is the most common method and produces the most consistent results. Salt used should be kosher, pickling, and canning, or flake salt. Do not use iodized, rock, or sea salt. These may contain impurities and can cause an off-flavor. Herbs and spices are often added to the brine for flavor. Commercial fish brines are also available, again with a variety of spices and herbs. Cure may or may not be used, depending on the recipe.

A general-purpose brine consists of 1 part salt to 7 parts of water, or 1 cup of salt to 7 cups of water. Make the brine using ice water, or chill the brine to 38°F or lower before using. This will help the flesh take up the salt and reduce bacterial growth. Make sure you have

enough chilled brine to cover the fish. Place the fish in the brine, making sure it is well submerged, and brine for anywhere from ½ to 6 hours, or for the time suggested by the recipe.

Equalizing

Remove the fish from the brine and wash thoroughly. Soak for about an hour in fresh cold water to remove excess brine. The fish must be dried and the salt equalized. This allows the salt to be evenly distributed throughout the fish. The fish should also be allowed to

ABOVE: The brines are made using ice water or by chilling the brine before use, and then submerging the fish in the brine.

dry so the surface forms a tough, shiny coat, or pellicle. This seals in the moisture and provides an evenly smoked appearance without streaks. Keep the fish refrigerated at temperatures below 38°F for salt equalization and to begin the surface-drying process. This may take from 2 to 24 hours, depending on species, recipe, and thickness of the pieces. Normally, 1-inch-thick fillets will take from 6 to 10 hours.

BELOW: The fish is removed from the brine, laid on a paper towel, and patted dry.

ABOVE: Fish is then hot-smoked. In days past, fish were often cold-smoked, along with salting for preservation. These days, the suggested method is to hot-smoke only to an internal temperature of 160°F.

Smoking

Smoking may be done in water-pan smokers, large barbecue smokers, as well as dedicated wood or electric smokers. Forming the pellicle, or outer coating, usually requires a warmer temperature. This is normally done in the smoker before the smoking begins. A low temperature without smoke is used, and may take from 30 minutes to 2 hours. After the pellicle has formed, the fish is smoked. Two basic methods are used: cold smoke and hot smoke. Hot smoke may be indirect- or direct- heat smoke cooking.

Cold-smoking fish is actually drying out the meat, resulting in an internal temperature of less than 90 degrees. Examples are lox or Nova Scotia–style salmon. Cold smoking results in raw fish, and steps must be taken to kill bacteria and parasites. Cold smoking is difficult in areas with a high humidity and requires long smoking times or several days.

Hot smoking is the most popular form with home fish smokers. Hot smoking may be done with a dedicated smoker, either wood or electric. After the pellicle has formed, the temperature of the smoker is gradually raised to 160°F. Raising temperatures too quickly can cause the fish pieces to break apart. The final smoker temperature should be from 180°F to 225°F, depending on the recipe. The fish should be cooked to an internal temperature of 160°F and held at that temperature for at least 30 minutes, and this should occur within 6 to 8 hours of placing the meat in the smoker. Use a standard meat thermometer or remote thermometer placed in the thickest portion of the fish to test. If the smoker doesn't raise the temperature properly within 8 hours or so, continue cooking the smoked fish in a home oven set at 300°F for final heat treatment. Again, bring the internal temperature to 160°F and bake for at least 30 minutes.

The second method of hot smoking is direct smoke cooking, such as done on a barbecue grill or water-pan smoker. In this case, the smoke-cooking temperatures are usually higher, and smoking times are much shorter.

Storage

Proper storage of smoked fish is also important. Allow the smoked or heated fish to cool at room temperature. Then wrap in plastic wrap and keep refrigerated at below 38°F. The smoked fish can also be pressure-canned, frozen, or, better yet, vacuum-packed and frozen.

Smoked Fish Recipes

Bradley Maple Cured Smoked Salmon

Bradley Smoker is famous for their salmon smoking, and their maple-flavored salmon is excellent served with wild rice and stir-fried vegetables. Or smash and blend with equal amounts of cream cheese for a delicious spread.

1 large salmon fillet	¼ cup lemon juice
1 quart water	10 whole cloves
½ cup pickling and canning salt	10 whole allspice berries
½ cup maple syrup	1 bay leaf
¼ cup dark rum	

In a medium-sized bowl, combine the brine ingredients. Place the salmon fillet in a nonmetallic dish and cover with the brine. Make certain the fish is completely submersed in the brine. Cover and refrigerate for at least 2 hours. Remove salmon from the brine and pat dry with paper towels. Place salmon skin-side down on smoker rack and allow to air-dry for about 1 hour.

Preheat the Bradley smoker to between 180°F and 200°F. Using Bradley maple-flavor bisquettes, smoke-cook the salmon approximately 1 ½ hours.

Hi Mountain Alaskan Salmon Brine Mix

Another maple-flavored recipe, this utilizes a maple-flavored and spiced brine. The package comes with two pouches of cure. Dissolve 1 pouch in 1 gallon of ice water. Fish should be fresh and chilled before curing. Immerse the fish in the brine solution, making sure it is completely covered. Place in a refrigerator for 24 hours.

Remove fish from the brine, rinse well with fresh cold water, and pat dry. Let fish sit at room temperature for about 30 minutes, then smoke. Smoking time can vary depending on the type of smoker, location, outside temperature, and so forth. Fish should be smoked until internal temperature reaches 155°F to 160°F.

Bradley's Famous Hot-Smoked Salmon

If you luck into a cooler full of salmon, this recipe is a good choice, and it has been one of Bradley's most popular recipes using their alder bisquettes.

Cure (white sugar and salt—approximately 1 pound of salt to 2 ounces of sugar)	Coarse ground black pepper
	Dried parsley or chive flakes
Vegetable oil	
Garlic and onion salt or powder (You can substitute dill or dry mustard for the garlic and onion.)	

Leave the skin on the salmon. If fillet is over 1 inch thick, slash the flesh every 2 to 3 inches about ½ to ⅜ inch deep, parallel and running in the direction of the rib. Slather fish with a liberal amount of vegetable oil. Sprinkle cure heavily and evenly on the fillet. Use enough cure so that it doesn't wet out in the oil. Sprinkle a moderate amount of desired spices over the fillet. Rub the spices and cure lightly, including any cut surfaces. Sprinkle a moderate amount of coarse black pepper. Wrap two similar-sized salmon fillets, flesh to flesh, with plastic wrap or plastic bag and then place in a cooler or nonmetallic container. Cover fish to ensure air has no access and refrigerate 14 to 20 hours.

Remove fish from the cure and place skin-side down on oiled racks. Rub fillets to even out the residual cure and sprinkle with parsley or chive flakes. Place the racks in the Bradley smoker. Using alder-flavored bisquettes, start the Bradley smoker at a very low temperature (100°F to 120°F) for 1 to 2 hours. After the first 2 hours, increase the temperature to 140° F for 2 to 4 hours. Finish at 175°F to 200°F for 1 to 2 hours.

Smoked Blue Cats

Blue cats can get big, well over 100 pounds, and these big cats can provide large fillets, excellent for smoking. Their flaky, white, but somewhat oily flesh provides a good smoked flavor. The skins should be removed and the fillets trimmed so the meat is an even thickness, cutting away some of the thin belly meat as well as the thinner portion of the tail area. Make up enough brine to cover and submerge the fillets. One gallon of brine will do about 5 pounds of fillets.

1 gallon ice water	1 tsp. garlic powder
1 cup brown sugar	1 tsp. onion powder
½ cup canning or pickling salt	1 tsp. ground red pepper
½ cup soy sauce	1 tsp. ground black pepper
¼ cup Worcestershire sauce	

Add the brine ingredients to the gallon of water and heat to dissolve all ingredients. Chill brine and pour over cleaned fillets in a noncorrosive plastic container. Weight the fillets to keep them well submerged. An alternative method is to place the fish and brine in a sealable plastic food bag, and then place this in a container in case the bag leaks. The double-fastening–type bag works best for this tactic. Two-gallon freezer bags will hold the brine and about 5 or 6 pounds of fillets. Place in a refrigerator and leave for about 4 hours at 38°F. Turn the bags or move the fillets around once an hour to make sure the brine is evenly distributed.

Remove from the brine and place on paper towels. Pat dry, then place on smoker racks or other raised racks. Allow to air-dry at room temperature for an hour or so. The surface of the fish should start to become slightly hard, forming a pellicle. Or dry in the smoker with the smoker set at an extremely low temperature.

Gradually increase the temperature to 180°F or 200°F and cook until the fish flakes and the internal temperature reaches 160°F. Remove and cool the fish before serving.

Shake 'n' Smoke Salmon

This is a very simple and easy salmon recipe, but it can also be used with almost any fish. It's a great way of curing and smoking small fillets, such as bluegill.

Simply skin, clean, and prepare the fillets. Pat the fillets dry with paper towels. Place a cup of Morton Salt Sugar Cure mix and a cup of brown sugar in a large plastic food bag. Place the fillets a few at a time into the bag and shake to coat all surfaces. Remove and place in a noncorrosive or plastic bowl and place in the refrigerator for an hour. Remove, rinse in cold water, pat dry, and smoke in your smoker. You can also sprinkle liquid smoke over the cure-covered fillets and simply place them on wire racks in a 325-degree oven until done. Add your favorite seasonings and spices for added flavor.

Smoked Kings

Actually, any salmon can be used with this delicious recipe, but it's great with the big kings, also called chinook. The following brine will cure about 4 to 5 pounds of salmon.

3 quarts cold water	½ cup honey
I quart soy sauce	I tsp. garlic powder
2 cups brown sugar	I tsp. onion powder
I cup pickling or canning salt	I tbsp. ground white pepper

Mix ingredients in a saucepan, heat and stir until dissolved, and then chill in a refrigerator. Place salmon chunks in the brine in a noncorrosive container in the refrigerator. Salmon less than 1 inch thick will brine in 6 to 8 hours. Salmon 1 inch or more thick will require 12 hours' or overnight brining.

Remove from the brine, rinse, allow to air-dry for a couple of hours, and then hot-smoke to an internal temperature of 160°F.

Lemon Pepper Smoked Striper

The oily-white meat of ocean-run or inland stripers is a great choice for smoking. Large white bass or hybrids also have an oily flesh and can also be smoked. Prepare the fish by filleting and cutting into chunks.

I gallon water	I tsp. garlic powder
2 cups brown sugar	I tsp. onion powder
½ cup salt	½ tsp. ginger
½ cup reconstituted lemon juice	I tbsp. lemon pepper

Place cleaned and prepared fish chunks in chilled brine overnight in a refrigerator that is cooler than 38°F. Remove from the brine and rinse the fish in cold water. Dry the fish and hot-smoke until the internal temperature reaches 160°F.

Hot-Smoked Bluefish

If you have an abundance of blues, and who doesn't when the bite is on, this is a great recipe for doing 20 or so pounds of fish. Clean the fish and cut into equal-sized fillets, leaving the skins on. Make up the brine to cover fish, using ½ pound salt and 1 pound of brown sugar to each gallon of water needed to cover the fish. Brine overnight in a refrigerator. Remove from the brine, rinse, and pat dry. Place on smoker racks with the skin-side down and hot-smoke until an internal temperature of 160°F is reached. With a temperature-controlled smoker, this should average 4 hours at 120°F, plus 2 hours at 180 degrees.

Smoked Tuna Steaks

Tuna steaks are also great salted and smoked. Cover with the following brine:

½ gallon water	I tsp. reconstituted lemon juice
½ cup salt	I tbsp. ground white pepper
I cup brown sugar	¼ tsp. ground ginger
6 bay leaves (crumbled)	

Mix ingredients in water, simmer until dissolved, and then chill the brine. Place tuna steaks in a large plastic sealable food bag, add chilled brine, and place in a refrigerator for 4 hours. Turn once every hour.

Remove from the brine, rinse, pat dry, and allow to air-dry for about a half hour. Brush with vegetable oil and place in smoker. This is an excellent recipe to use with a water smoker. Just add white wine to the water pan. Smoke for 3 or 4 hours, or until tender and flaky.

Smoked Oysters

If you want a real treat, try smoked oysters. This recipe is for ½ gallon of oysters. Rinse the oysters and drain them in a colander. While the oysters are draining, prepare the brine.

2 quarts water	I cup brown sugar
I cup soy sauce	I tsp. onion powder
½ cup salt	I tsp. garlic powder

Stir the ingredients into the water, simmer, and stir until all ingredients are dissolved. Bring to a boil and add the oysters. Cook for 10 to 30 minutes. Remove the cooked oysters and drain in a colander.

Hot-smoke the oysters in a smoker for 4 to 6 hours for added flavor.

Smoked Smelt

Smelt are excellent smoked and make great appetizers. Cure and smoke same as for larger fish, but do not brine very long, about an hour or two, and then wash thoroughly in fresh water. Smoke the smelt until they turn a golden brown and are completely cooked. Allow to cool before serving. The bones and all are eaten and make a delicious appetizer or meal.

Smoked Eel

A delicious but, granted, fairly localized, smoked product, eel can be skinned and filleted for smoking, but it is traditionally smoked whole. Freshly killed eels should be washed in clean, cold water and scraped to remove slime. You may need to repeat this step several times to remove all traces of slime. Another method to deslime eel is to simply cover them with salt in a noncorrosive container. Eviscerate the eel and remove all traces of blood. Soak the eel in 80 percent brine for 30 minutes to 1 hour. Allow to dry thoroughly and then hang from rods in the smoker. Place small sticks between the belly flaps to keep them open. Smoke at 100°F to 120°F for 1 hour, raise the temperature gradually to 140°F, and then gradually to 180°F or 200°F, and smoke until an internal temperature of 160°F is reached.

Pickled Fish

Although salt is applied, pickling fish is not the same as curing in brine and then drying. Almost any type of fish can be pickled, but traditional favorites include herring and carp. Pickled fish is not cooked and should be frozen at 0°F for two weeks or longer to get rid of any parasites. Check your freezer to make sure the temperature is cold enough. Pickled fish is also only mildly preserved and must be kept refrigerated.

Eviscerate and wash the fish in clean, cold water. Remove fins, tail, and head. Scale or skin, then cut into 1-inch-thick pieces. Soak the pieces in brine made of 1 gallon of water with 2 cups of salt dissolved in the water.

While the fish are soaking, make up a pickling mix (leaving out the onion). Use the proportions below to make up a pickling mix sufficient to cover the fish. Bring the mix to a boil and set aside to cool before using.

1½ quarts distilled white vinegar	6 bay leaves
2½ pints water	¼ cup reconstituted lemon juice
1 tsp. whole allspice	½ cup brown sugar
1 tbsp. mixed pickling spices	1 large onion (sliced)
1 tsp. mustard seed	

Drain fish from brine and pack in clean, sterilized glass jars. Place onion slices in jars and pour cooled pickling mix over. Place lids on the jars and shake well to distribute the spices. Keep refrigerated and use within 6 to 8 weeks.

9

Wild Game Recipes

FOR MANY HUNTERS, salt curing and smoking is a favorite means of preserving or, more commonly, cooking game, including venison, big game, and game birds. As with other types of meats, different methods of cure application can be used, depending on the cut of meat and the desired end result. This includes dry cure and injection cure or stitch or artery pumping, or a combination of the methods. Small cuts, such as loins and cuts from the hams and shoulders, are commonly cured using the dry-cure method. Larger pieces, such as hams, are best cured with a combination of dry cure and injection. Salt-cured game meats may or may not be smoked, but all must be hot-smoked or cooked. As with all meats, it's important to start with clean, fresh, safe, and well-chilled meat.

Corned Deer Loin

The loin is one of our favorite cuts to corn. It tastes almost like corned beef, with a mild game flavor, and there is no fat to be removed. It is, however, a bit dryer because there are no connective fat tissues or marbling. This recipe is easy using Morton Salt Tender Quick.

ABOVE: Venison and other big game meats can be corned as easily as beef. The same methods are used.

5 lb. deer loin, boneless venison roast, or combination	6 tbsp. Morton Tender Quick
	1 tbsp. garlic powder
2 to 3 quarts water, to cover	1 tbsp. onion powder
1 cup brown sugar	2 tbsp. mixed pickling spices

Place the brine ingredients in a large saucepan. Bring to a boil, reduce to simmer, and stir until all ingredients are dissolved. Place in a large food-grade plastic container and place in the refrigerator to chill. Once chilled, add the chilled meat, cover the container, and keep refrigerated 5 to 7 days, depending on the thickness of the meat. Turn the meat once each day. Remove, wash in cold running water, and place in a large pot. Cover with water and simmer for 3 to 4 hours. Remove, chill, thin-slice, and serve. This makes an excellent Reuben sandwich. Freeze excess for future use in vacuum- seal bags.

Venison Ham

A cured ham from a deer is mighty tasty. The cured deer ham can be smoke-cooked, oven-roasted, or boiled. A deer ham is best cured using the combination dry cure and injection. The same basic recipes and techniques for curing a pork ham can also be used on a deer ham. In this case, the deer ham is cut from the carcass by making a cut similar to that for long-cut pork ham, cutting through the aitchbone and pelvic arch.

Trim and smooth up the butt end and cut off the shank fairly short, as the shank of a deer has little meat. A simple method is to use Morton Salt Sugar Cure (Plain) mix. Make up the sweet pickle cure first by combining one cup of the Morton Salt Sugar Cure (Plain) mix with 4 cups of clean, cool water and mix until dissolved. Weigh the ham and make up enough pickle to have 1 ounce of pickle for each pound of meat. Pump the pickle into the ham, using a meat pump and injecting along the bone structure. After the ham has been pumped, apply a dry cure to the meat surface. Again, Morton Salt Sugar Cure (Plain) mix makes the chore easy. Since deer hams are usually not aged, use 1 tablespoon of mix per pound of meat. Measure out enough cure mix to do the ham and divide into 3 equal parts. Apply ⅓ of the mix on the first day and place in a large covered food-grade plastic

BELOW: A ham from a deer can also be salt-cured just like a pork ham. The best method is the combination-cure method of injecting a pickle cure along with using the dry-cure method.

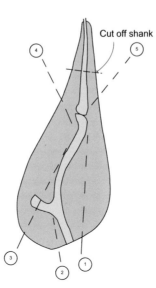

container or bag and then place in a refrigerator with a temperature of 38°F. After 7 days, apply another third of the cure, and then on day 14, apply the last third. The deer ham should be cured after 14 to 15 days, followed by an equalization period.

To equalize, remove from the container and soak the ham for about an hour in clean, cold water. Lightly scrub off the excess cure and place in a clean food-grade plastic bag or container. Place in the refrigerator and allow the salt to equalize throughout the ham. This will take about 14 days. Remove from the bag, soak again in cold water, and then hang to dry. The ham can be smoked or cooked, but the ham must be heat-treated to 160°F internally before being consumed.

Bacon Smoked Quail

If you're looking for a unique quail dish, this is it. The same recipe can be used with pheasant, quail, or chukars. First step is to make up a weak brine solution.

1 quart water	1 tsp. onion powder
3 tbsp. non-iodized salt	1 tsp. garlic powder
1 tbsp. lemon juice concentrate	1 tsp. black pepper
1 tsp. dried parsley	½ tsp. paprika

Dissolve the salt and spices in the heated water, then place the brine in the refrigerator to cool. Place the cleaned whole birds in a food-grade plastic bag and pour the mixed (cold) brine into the bag. Place in a plastic food container and place in a refrigerator. Allow to cure for 4 to 6 hours, turning frequently to make sure all pieces are thoroughly soaked.

Remove, rinse the brine, and place on paper towels. Pat the birds dry with paper towels. Drape bacon pieces over the breast of the birds and pin in place with toothpicks. Smoke using apple or alder at 200°F to 225°F until the internal temperature reaches 165°F.

ABOVE: Upland game—such as quail, pheasant, and chukars—can all be lightly brined and smoked. Clean thoroughly, removing all feathers and pinfeathers. Cut off feet. Dig out any shot and cut away any bloody areas.

BELOW: Cure upland birds in a mild brine for 4 to 6 hours, then hot-smoke in a smoker with a water pan to an internal temperature of 170°F. Bacon strips added across the breast can add moistness.

Apple-Soaked Mallard Breasts

Just about any duck can be used—including teal, wood ducks, and gadwalls, one of my favorite eating ducks. The bigger ducks provide a more moist breast, and of course, more meat. Breast out the ducks and remove the breast skin. Cut away any bloody areas and dig out any shot. Steel shot can be mighty hard on the teeth. Prepare the following brine, and soak the breast overnight. This will brine about 2 pounds of duck breasts, or the breasts from 2 mallards.

I quart water	2 bay leaves (crushed)
I can or jar applesauce	I tsp. garlic powder
3 tbsp. non-iodized salt	I tsp. onion powder
¼ to ½ cup brown sugar	I tbsp. lemon pepper

Thoroughly mix all ingredients, except for the lemon pepper, in hot water and allow the brine to cool. Place duck breasts and brine in a food-grade plastic container and leave overnight in the refrigerator. Remove from the brine, rinse, and dry with paper towels. Sprinkle each duck breast with lemon pepper and place bacon strips across the breasts. Secure in place with toothpicks. Smoke with applewood in a smoker at 225°F for a couple of hours. Duck is normally best eaten medium rare, but can be smoked until the internal temperature reaches 165°F. To keep duck breasts moist, place in aluminum foil after the first hour of smoking. Slice and serve with baked apples.

Smoked Sky Carp

Snow geese are called sky carp for good reason—they're plentiful, with large limits, tough to bag, and tough to cook. The meat is extremely dark and dry. Salt curing and smoking can, however, provide delicious goose meat, and is a good choice for the big Canada honkers as well. Only the breasts are used. Remove the breasts and remove the skins. Clean up any bloody spots and remove all steel shot. Slice the breasts into ½-inch strips. Make the following brine and soak the strips overnight in a refrigerator.

I cup soy sauce	2 tbsp. Worcestershire sauce
I cup water	I tsp. garlic powder
I cup brown sugar	I tsp. onion powder
2 tbsp. non-iodized salt	I tsp. ground red pepper, or to taste
I tbsp. black pepper	

Remove the strips, rinse under cold water, and dry on paper towels. Smoke using hickory at 200 to 225 degrees for a couple of hours, or until the internal temperature reaches 170°F. After the first hour of smoking, place the goose strips in aluminum foil to prevent drying.

Wild Game Summer Sausage

Summer sausage is an excellent way of salt-curing and smoking wild game meats. Although venison is probably the single most common meat used, just about any big game, small game, and waterfowl can be used to make summer sausage. The recipe used is easy, with Morton Salt Tender Quick mix. You will need some pork trimmings to add a little fat to the wild game meat. This is a good recipe to use with electric smokers.

3 lb. venison or other wild game	½ tsp. ground ginger
2 lb. pork trimmings	½ tsp. ground mustard
I tbsp. black pepper	I tsp. garlic powder
5 tbsp. Morton Tender Quick mix	4 tbsp. corn syrup
I tsp. ground coriander	

Weigh the meats separately. Cut chilled meat into 1-inch cubes and grind through a 3/16-inch grinder plate. Mix the dry spice ingredients in a glass bowl and sprinkle over the ground meat. Dribble the

Wild game can also be used to create great-tasting summer sausages. Smoking in an electric smoker adds to the flavor.

corn syrup over the ground meat and thoroughly mix all. Place in a plastic or glass bowl and refrigerate overnight. Spread the meat out to about a 1-inch depth in a shallow, flat pan and freeze for an hour or so or until the meat is partially frozen. Remove and regrind the partially frozen meat through a ⅛-inch plate. Stuff the ground meat into synthetic casings. If your meat grinder has a stuffing attachment, the final grinding and stuffing can be done in one step.

Hang the stuffed casings on drying racks and dry at room temperature for 4 to 5 hours, or hang in a smoker on sticks, with the damper open until the casings are dry to the touch. Set the temperature of the smoker to 120°F or 130°F, add wood chips, and smoke for 3 to 4 hours. Raise the temperature to 170°F and cook until the internal temperature reaches 165°F. Remove from the smoker and shower the casings with cold water. Place back in the cooled-down smoker and hang at room temperature for 1 to 3 hours or until dry. Freeze sausages that will not be consumed within a week. For more sausage recipes, see Monte Burch's *The Complete Guide to Sausage Making*.

PART III
Hot Smoking

COLD SMOKING TAKES place at temperatures of 80°F to 100°F. This imparts flavor but does not firm up the proteins in meats. All smoked meats must be hot-smoked or cooked before consumption, even those meats that are previously cold-smoked. Hot smoking at temperatures of 160°F to 225°F, or 250°F, provides flavor and cooks the meat.

Hot smoking of foods has become a popular American pastime, from the tailgaters at the ball games to the community whole-hog roast, and in backyard barbecues all over the country. Hot smoking is rather hard to define because it ranges from daylong slow smoking of ribs in an indirect-heat hot smoker to cooking a maple-glazed ham in

⑩
Hot Smoking Basics

an electric smoker to any number of foods hot-smoked using a water smoker. With a little ingenuity, even the popular barbecue grill can be used to hot-smoke in addition to grilling. A wide range of foods can be hot-smoked, including all varieties of meats as well as vegetables, and even some fruits. Some of this type of hot smoking falls into the realm of grilling or direct-heat cooking.

The hot-smoking techniques depend on your equipment, the type of meat, and the recipe chosen. Two methods are used for all hot smoking—direct and indirect cooking. Direct cooking is cooking directly above the heat source, such as with a barbecue grill. This type of cooking is the best choice for fast-cooking foods such

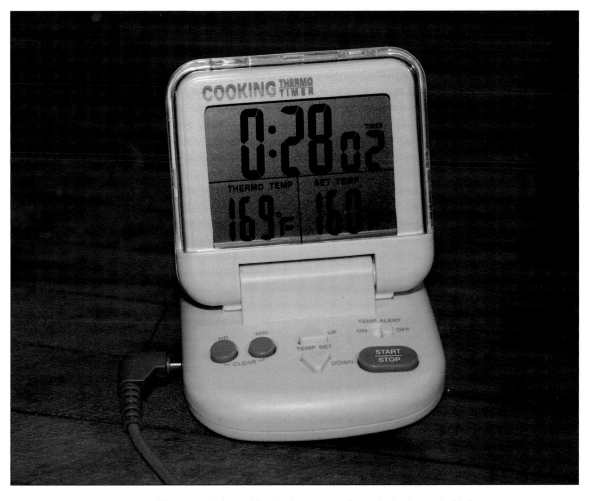

ABOVE: All meats, including cold-smoked meats, must be cooked or hot-smoked before consumption. The internal temperature reached depends on the meat smoked.

as steaks, chops, frankfurters, fish fillets, and hamburgers as well as some vegetables. In most instances, charcoal briquettes or gas is used as the heat source. Wood chips can be added to provide the smoke flavor. As with broiling, foods are seared and cooked quickly. In indirect cooking, foods are cooked by reflected heat. This is the method used with dedicated wood or charcoal smokers, which have the firebox off to one side from the cooking surface. Indirect cooking

ABOVE: Hot smoking may be by direct or indirect heat. The type of hot smoking or cooking depends on the type of smoker or cooker used.

can also be done using a barbecue grill by placing foods like chicken, ribs, fish, and sausages on one side of the grill and applying heat to the opposite side. Place a foil drip pan under the food.

Another method is to place large cuts of meat, such as a pork shoulder or whole birds, on a roast rack in a drip pan. Cover and cook. These methods do require a good-quality covered grill and require more cooking time. You can also combine the two methods, first searing the meats over direct heat and then moving it away from the heat and cooking more slowly by indirect heat. Brush the meat with sauce or marinade during the final cooking stages.

Water smoking is another technique. In this case, a water pan is placed between the food and the heat source. This creates a moist cloud and keeps the meat moist and juicy. Any number of liquids can be used in the water pan to add flavor, including sweetened fruit juices, beer, wine, and herbs and spices. Liquid smoke can be added to the pan to provide an easy-does-it smoking technique. Wood chips add even more aroma and flavor. Most indirect and water-pan cooking techniques (hot smoking) are slow methods. Cooking time can range from an hour or so to 10 or 12 hours, depending on the smoker, meats, and recipe.

Fuel Types

Hot smoking and/or grilling can be done with wood chunks, charcoal, or gas, with the addition of wood chips. These days many smokers utilize wood pellets. We've covered woods for cold smoking in the previous chapters. Basically, the same woods are used, but with some differences.

The larger, dedicated, indirect-heat smokers can utilize charcoal or wood chunks. Many purists prefer wood chunks. Charcoal can be used in many of these units, but the fire will not get as hot as with chunks of natural wood. These big chunks are easier to use once you get your fire started, last longer, and naturally impart plenty of smoke for cooking and flavoring.

As with the wood chips used in cold smoking, it's important to use the proper wood. Any of the fruited hardwoods—such as white oak,

Smoking requires fuel and/or wood of some sort. Wood chips are commonly used in electric and gas- and charcoal-fueled smokers to add the flavor.

hickory, and pecan—are good. Red oak sometimes provides a bitter flavor and it's easy to overly smoke with this flavor. The fruitwoods—including apple, peach, cherry, pear, and apricot—are also excellent choices. With lots of timber and oak and hickory trees on our property, we have plenty of smoking wood. We also have a big apple orchard, and our favorite smoking wood is the pruning pieces from the apple trees. Other popular choices include mesquite and alder. We've experimented with just about every smokable wood available, and our favorites include hickory for beef and apple for pork, chicken, and fish. Never use cedar, pine, or kiln-dried wood chunks.

The makers of Horizon Smokers also suggest any wood used for smoking in their units should be cured for at least a year.

BELOW: Some smokers suggest soaking the chips in water for an hour before using.

ABOVE: Some smokers utilize wood chunks instead of chips.

Green wood still has all the sap and moisture that once kept the tree alive. When you burn it, the sap produces a super-strong-tasting smoke and turns your meat black. Also, when you try burning green wood, it is hard to reach a good temperature because all the moisture inside the wood attempts to extinguish the fire while it is burning. Cured wood lights easily and will maintain a steady cooking temperature for several hours with very little maintenance. Also, cured wood produces a good-tasting smoke flavor that isn't overpowering.

Acquiring amounts of seasoned chunk wood is not as easy as buying a bag of charcoal. You may need to scout around for sources. You also should experiment with the sizes of chunk wood your smoker utilizes best. With a small chain saw, you can sometimes acquire salvaged smoking wood from storm-damaged trees, or from the slash or treetops left by loggers. A maul is also necessary for splitting the wood into smaller pieces. The best sizes for most smokers are log sections 6 to 12 inches long and 2 to 3 inches in diameter. A 4- to 6-inch log split into quarters is an excellent choice. Be sure to cure the wood for a year, keeping it stored in a dry place and up off the ground. You will also need smaller pieces for starting fires.

Lighting a fire in a wood smoker, such as the Horizon, is similar to starting a good campfire or fireplace fire. With tinder or fine light wood pieces that will light easily with a match, you really won't need any artificial starter, although flammable fire sticks used for campfire starting can be used. Do not use charcoal lighter. Build the

BELOW: Larger, dedicated, indirect-heat smokers are best fueled with wood logs and chunks, the wood supplying both the heat and smoke. Use only woods from fruit and nut trees; do not use resinous woods.

fire properly before lighting it. Open both dampers on the smoker and lay a couple of small logs in the firebox, and to both sides. Place tinder across the logs and place small pieces of wood that will burn easily before the tinder burns away across the tinder. Place a few larger pieces of wood across the smaller pieces, but make sure to leave gaps between all the wood pieces to allow air through the wood and channel the heat from the burning tinder upward through the wood pieces. This creates a small chimney to make the fire "draw." On a larger scale, this is known as the stack effect and is exactly why smokers such as the Horizon have a built-in smokestack. Open the

firebox damper and the stack damper completely. Crumple a piece of newspaper and place under the tinder. Light the fire. With stacking practice and the right materials, a smoker fire will light with one match.

Allow your fire time to build properly and bring your smoker up to temperature before attempting to cook. It's a bad idea to try to cook in a cold smoker, or to keep trying to nurse a fire into life while you're attempting to cook. Wait until the fire has burned for a period of time and needs little maintenance before attempting to cook. As the heat inside the smoker rises into the smokestack, it pulls cooler air in behind it to provide oxygen to the fire. This air, heated by the fire, rises up the smokestack. Once the fire is burning good and the smoker reaches the desired temperature, and with adequate fire maintenance materials in the firebox, partially close the dampers. Check the temperature in a few minutes. The higher the desired cooking temperature, the wider the damper openings need to be. Adjust the two dampers to fine-tune the setting. Once the desired setting is obtained, the smoker will require your attention only occasionally. If, however, your fire has been left too long and has burned down to coals, pull the coals together and add more sticks of seasoned wood, opening the dampers to increase the air supply. Do not smother the coals with too much wood too quickly.

Charcoal is a favorite of many hot smokers and grillers. Charcoal is more readily available than seasoned wood and provides smoke-flavored cooking. Charcoal is available as briquettes or as lump charcoal. Each has its advantages and disadvantages. The main difference between the two is that lump charcoal is basically whole pieces of wood that have been heated to high temperatures without oxygen, leaving only the carbon matter. In briquettes the carbon is processed further—ground up, mixed with a variety of fillers, and then compressed into briquette shapes.

Lump charcoal is extremely clean burning. If burned in a grill or smoker without air control, and with free oxygen, it's also extremely hot and fast burning. Some brands can burn as hot as 1,000 degrees, producing a fire that's much too hot for most smoking, but ideal for flash-grilling steaks. The burn rate of lump charcoal can, however, be regulated with a smoker or grill with good air control. Different brands of lump charcoal also have different burn rates or burn times and heat output. The lumps are made of chunks of wood, and unlike briquettes, the sizes of the chunks vary. The size and distribution of sizes in a bag also varies from brand to brand. You'll have to experiment to find the brand that works best for you.

Some lump charcoal is made from pieces of wood in its natural state—branches, limbs, and pieces of log, or scraps from sawmilling. Some lump charcoal is made from kiln-dried lumber scraps, which may be scraps from cabinets, trim and molding, and flooring manufactures. Most lump charcoal is made from hardwoods, but not all. In some instances, plywood—which contains glues and wood scraps that have been finished—is included, and this is not good for you or the environment. Use only a good-quality, hardwood lump charcoal.

Like all charcoal, lump charcoal is fairly easy to light. Although charcoal lighter can be used, an electric charcoal starter and charcoal chimney are the best choices. I prefer a charcoal chimney for lighting all types of charcoal. There are no off-flavors from the charcoal lighter fluid, and a charcoal chimney is easy to use. Place two sheets of crumpled-up newspaper in the bottom, and place the chimney on a safe, noncombustible surface. Add the lumps and light the newspaper. You may have to add and light several more sheets of newspaper to get the charcoal started, but when the flames begin to rise through

Charcoal is a very common and economical fuel for smoke cooking. It is available in both lump and briquette form.

the chimney, the lumps are lit. Once the bottom pieces are lit, an updraft is created, bringing more air and oxygen across the charcoal, rapidly lighting all the chunks.

If you're using the lump charcoal for slow smoke cooking in your grill or smoker, first, place a pile of unlit chunks in the smoker or grill. Pour the started hot lumps over the unlit pieces. As the charcoal burns down, the lumps on top starting those below it, a low, steady heat is created for a period of time. To create smoke, add wood chips of your favorite flavor to the pile of unlit lumps before adding the started pieces.

Briquettes, however, are the most common type of charcoal used for smoking and grilling. They're readily available, easy to start, and relatively slow burning. Briquettes are available as standard, instant lighting, and even "gourmet-style," with smoking woods added. These make it extremely easy to smoke-cook, without the hassle of adding chips. Available in 5-, 10-, and 25-pound bags, the different brands provide varying degrees of heat. Briquettes are basically made from sawdust and wood scraps that are burned into carbon. This is then compressed along with ground coal and a binder into a uniformly shaped product that burns with a slow, nice, even heat. Believe it or not, Henry Ford started the first briquette factory, Kingsford, to get rid of wood scraps from the production of his Model T automobiles. Some purists do not like to use briquettes because they contain the binders and fillers.

Briquettes are easy to light. The most common method is to simply stack them in the smoker or grill in pyramid fashion. If indirect smoke cooking, place the briquette pile off to one side of the smoker or grill food grate. Apply charcoal starter fluid to the pile. Let the pile sit for about a minute and then light with match or electric lighter. Never add more charcoal lighter fluid to the briquettes after the fire is started. Paraffin fire starters can also be used. A charcoal chimney makes briquette starting easier and safer and doesn't add chemicals to your heat source. Instant-lighting charcoal briquettes require only a match to light. Caution: Some smoker manufacturers warn not

A charcoal chimney provides the best method of starting charcoal and doesn't add any off-flavors to the fire.

ABOVE: Charcoal is ready to use when a light coating of ash forms on the briquettes.

to use briquettes pretreated with lighter fluid; rather, use only stand-ard plain charcoal or charcoal wood mixture.

Once the briquettes are covered with a light ash, turning gray in sunlight or glowing red at night, you're ready to cook. This usu-ally takes about 20 to 30 minutes. Smoke-cooking different foods requires different cooking temperatures. A traditional method of determining heat when direct cooking with charcoal is to hold your hand, palm down, over the fire at cooking height. If you must remove your hand after 2 seconds, the temperature is high or hot; 3 seconds indicates a medium or high heat; 4 seconds a medium heat; and 5 sec-onds a low heat. This does not work with indirect cooking or smokers, and an internal smoker thermometer is necessary.

Regardless of whether you're using lump or briquette charcoal, proper storage is extremely important. Do not allow the charcoal to get wet. Briquettes will crumble and be hard to start. Charcoal may also pick up moisture if left in an opened bag. And the starter chemicals in instant-starting briquettes may evaporate. Fold the top of an opened bag over and then use clothesline clips or other large clips to keep the bag closed, or place in a bucket or tub with a tight-fitting lid.

Water Pan Smoking

Smoke cooking with water pan smokers, such as the Brinkmann smoker, is done with charcoal and flavored wood chips. Start the charcoal either with charcoal-starting fluid or in a charcoal chimney. If using a charcoal chimney starter, heed all manufacturer's warnings and instructions regarding the use of their product. Carefully place 8 to 10 pounds of hot coals in the charcoal pan.

If using charcoal-starting fluid, note all manufacturer's warnings and instructions regarding the use of their product. Use charcoal-lighting fluid approved for lighting charcoal *only*. Do not use gasoline, kerosene, or alcohol for lighting charcoal. Place 8 to 10 pounds of high-quality charcoal in the charcoal pan. Saturate the charcoal with lighting fluid, wait 2 to 3 minutes for the fluid to soak in. Carefully light the charcoal and allow to burn until covered with a light ash (approximately 20 minutes) prior to closing the door and placing the dome lid on the smoker. This will allow the charcoal-lighting fluid to burn off. Warning: Failure to do this could trap fumes from charcoal-lighting fluid in the smoker and may result in a flash fire or explosion when the door is opened or the dome lid is removed. An 8- to 10-pound pan of charcoal will burn 5 to 6 hours.

Add the smoke-flavoring wood to the started briquettes using long tongs. Wood chunks or sticks 3 to 4 inches long and ½ to ¾ inches thick work best. Unless the wood is still green, soak the wood in water for 20 minutes or wrap each piece in foil and tear several small holes in the foil to produce more smoke and prevent the wood from being consumed quickly. There is no need for a lot of wood to obtain a good smoke flavor. A recommended amount is 3 or 4 chunks

Water-pan, dome charcoal smokers are great for moist cooking and hot smoking.

or sticks. Experiment by using more wood for a stronger smoke flavor or less wood for milder flavor.

Place the water pan on the lower support brackets. Make sure it is resting securely on notched-out steps of all three support brackets. Carefully fill the water pan with warm water or marinade to 1 inch below the rim. A full pan holds 4 quarts or 1 gallon of liquid and will last 2 to 3 hours. Do not overfill and do not allow water to overflow from water pan.

Place a cooking grill on the lower support brackets directly on top of the water pan. Position the cooking grill so the rim is resting securely on the notched-out step of all three support brackets. Place food on the cooking grill in a single layer with space between each piece. This will allow smoke and moist heat to circulate evenly

BELOW: Water pans in many smokers can be filled with a marinade to add flavor.

around all pieces. Place the other cooking grill on the upper support brackets. Place food on the cooking grill.

After about 2 to 3 hours of smoke cooking, check the water and charcoal levels. Do not allow the liquid in the water pan to completely evaporate. Always keep the liquid in the water pan even after food is removed from the smoker. If the water evaporates before the fire cools completely, the grease in the water pan could catch fire. Always use a meat thermometer to ensure the food is fully cooked before removing from the smoker. Remove the dome lid by tilting it away from you so steam and heat escape away from your face. Add water through the top of the grill, or by opening the side door using a container with a long spout. Be careful not to splash water out of the pan. To add charcoal, remove dome lid and carefully open the side door. The door will

BELOW: In many instances, lining a charcoal smoker with aluminum foil adds to the effectiveness and cleanup.

be very hot, so use oven mitts and caution. Use long cooking tongs to lightly brush ashes off the hot coals, and then add charcoal and/or wood, being careful not to stir up ashes and sparks. Once charcoal is burning strong again, close the door and replace the dome lid.

Electric smokers capable of reaching cooking temperatures of 225°F to 250°F, such as Masterbuilt and Bradley, are excellent choices for hot smoking. Easily regulated, they're basically filled with meat, the temperature set, wood chips added, and then left alone. Even first-timers will have good results with these smokers.

Gas grill-smokers are also extremely popular. Either natural or propane-fueled, they take away the hassles of fire starting with either wood- or charcoal-fired cookers. Most of these units are used pri-

BELOW: Electric smokers can also hot-smoke, providing a great way of cooking pork roasts for pulled pork, as well as other dishes.

A big covered barbecue grill can also smoke by indirect heat.

READ INSTRUCTIONS BEFORE LIGHTING
1. Turn OFF gas burner control valves.
2. Turn ON gas source or tank.
3. Open lid during lighting.
4. To ignite, turn IGNITION BURNER knob to ⚡ HIGH.
5. Push and hold ELECTRONIC IGNITION button.
6. If ignition does NOT occur in 5 seconds, turn the burner controls off, wait 5 minutes, and

marily as grills for cooking with direct heat, but they can also be used as smokers as well with a little effort.

You need grill space large enough for indirect-heat cooking. In the past, many gas grills utilized lava rocks to help distribute the heat. Wood chips were placed on the lava rocks to create the smoke. Newer models these days have built-in heat tamers or heat-distribution plates that provide more even heating, improve the cleaning process, and reduce flare-ups. The addition of after-market lava rocks, charcoal, or briquettes of any type will cause poor combustion and increase the likelihood of a grease fire, and is not recommended. Using briquettes, lava rock, or charcoal in these grills will void the warranty.

A smoker box or pan with wood chips is used to add the desired smoke flavor. Smoke cooking with a gas grill unit is indirect cooking. Select burners are used to create and circulate heat throughout the grill, without direct contact between the meat and the flame. The meat is placed over the burner, or burners, that are off. This method can be used to slow-cook large cuts of meat and poultry. A pan is placed underneath the meat to catch grease and food drippings, and to help minimize cleanup.

To add the smoke, soak wood chips in water for approximately 30 minutes before adding to a smoke box or pan. Place the smoke box or pan on top of the cooking grate above the flame. Turn the burner on high until the wood starts to smoke. Reduce the heat to the desired temperature for cooking and place the food on the cooking grate for indirect cooking. Close the lid to retain the smoke.

Regardless of the type of smoke cooker, hot smoking is a hands-on experience. It is recommended you stay with your smoker or cooker and keep an eye on it, although frequently lifting a lid or opening a door only causes additional cooking time. Weather and ambient temperatures have a lot to do with cooking temperatures and cooking times, as do the thickness and type of meat. Wind is a real hassle, as it makes it hard to regulate temperatures. If you must cook in windy weather, keep the smoker on the downwind side of some sort of protection. Or create a wind shield or some sort of wind blocker. Of

ABOVE: Place a foil pouch of wood chips over the heat source.

course, rain can also be a real hassle. It's not unusual where we live in Missouri for a rainstorm to come up rather quickly, and if you are daylong smoking, it can be a real hassle. Do not, however, attempt to smoke or smoke-cook inside your garage or other buildings, even if you leave the doors wide open. Even if you don't burn the building down, you run the risk of death from carbon monoxide poisoning.

Cooking Temperatures

Different meats require different cooking temperatures and cooking times, and depending on whether you're indirect-hot smoking or direct-heat grilling.

Grilling Chart

Poultry: Use medium to low heat until flesh is no longer pink and joints move easily. Baste frequently and turn with tongs. Grill chicken pieces approximately 45 minutes, whole birds approximately 15 minutes per pound. Use a rotisserie for large birds.

Beef: Burgers and steaks should be seared quickly over medium hot coals, and then finished over medium coals. For burgers, use a grill basket and use tongs, not a fork, to turn steaks. Forks pierce the meat and allow juices to escape. For rare steaks, cook 7 minutes per

BELOW: Use a meat thermometer to smoke-cook meats to the proper internal temperature.

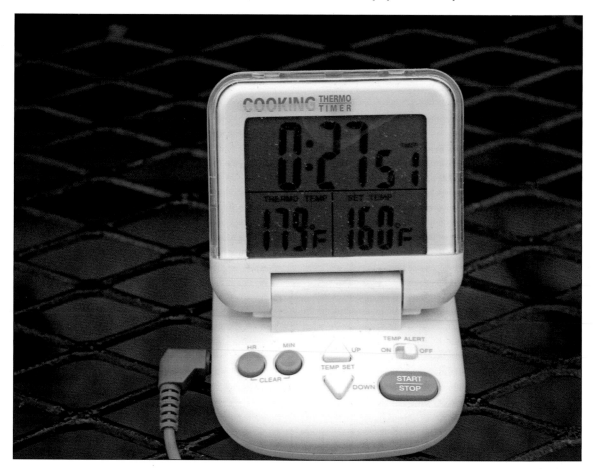

side; for medium 8 to 9 minutes per side. Roasts should be cooked using indirect heat over medium low heat, or use a rotisserie.

Pork: Cook with low to moderate heat slowly. Use indirect heat for roasts, or use water-pan cookers.

Fish: Cook for 10 minutes per inch of thickness over hot coals. Baste frequently to keep moist. Fish is done when the flesh flakes easily with a fork and is opaque.

You can also gauge the doneness of meat by the internal temperature: In most instances, the meat will further cook for a few minutes after removal from the grill.

Rare: 135°F
Medium rare: 140°F
Medium: 150°F
Well done: 165°F

Regardless of the meat or cooking method, always use a probe or digital meat thermometer to check the internal temperature of cooked meat and follow US Department of Agriculture's recommended safe minimum internal temperatures.

USDA Recommended Safe Minimum Internal Temperatures

Beef, veal, lamb, steaks, and roasts: 145°F
Fish: 145°F
Pork: 160°F
Beef, veal lamb, ground: 160°F
Turkey, chicken, and duck whole, pieces, and ground: 165°F.

MANY MEATS ARE first treated with a dry rub before they are smoked. Some recipes call for soaking the meats in a marinade. Or a sauce may be used by itself or combined with a rub or marinade. Any number of commercially prepared rubs, marinades, and sauces are available. You can, however, easily make up your own, creating your own special flavored smoke-cooked meats. Following are some of our favorite recipes for all types of hot-smoke cooking.

Rubs

Dry rubs consist of a variety of spices, herbs, salt, and pepper. Rubs are literally rubbed onto the meat prior to cooking. Following

11

Rubs, Sauces, and Marinades

are some tried-and-tested recipes. If you or your family don't like some of the ingredients, simply omit them and add what you do like. That's the joy of smoke cooking. Try your hand at mixing up different rub recipes. Mix all the herbs and spices in a bowl. If you're making more than needed for immediate use, store in covered plastic food containers, labeled as to the contents. When you find a rub you like, make up a big batch and store in plastic food containers for future use.

When applying the rub to the raw meat, spoon the rub on and don't let the spoon touch the meat in order not to cross-contaminate. Then use your fingers to rub the mixture over the meat surface. Cover the meat and let it sit for about 30 minutes.

ABOVE: A dry rub is often applied to meats before hot smoking. You can make up your own dry rub quite easily.

Simple Rub

It doesn't get any simpler than this. Start with this basic mix and add your favorite herbs or spices to create your own rub.

1 tbsp. salt	1 tbsp. chili powder
1 tbsp. black pepper	

Spicy Rub

This will make up about a cup of rub, enough for one brisket, rib slab, or two chickens; and it works equally well with all of them. A paprika-based rub, although it sounds hot, really isn't, but it does have a kick. Lessen the ground red pepper if you find it too hot.

¾ cup paprika

1 tbsp. crushed red pepper

1 tsp. ground red pepper

1 tbsp. chili powder

1 tbsp. lemon pepper

1 tbsp. ground black pepper

1 tsp. onion powder

1 tsp. garlic powder

1 tsp. celery salt

1 tsp. dry mustard

1 tbsp. dried basil

¼ tsp. turmeric

¼ tsp. cumin

Kansas City–Style Rub

Kansas City is famous for its smoke-cooked barbecues. The following rub will do for just about any smoke-cooked meat, but is especially good with pork ribs, pulled pork, and brisket. This recipe makes up a good-sized batch of rub, so you can try it on several different meats.

1½ cups salt

1½ cups ground black pepper

1½ cups brown sugar

1½ cups paprika

4 tsp. chili powder

1 tsp. ground red pepper

2 tsp. dry mustard

1 tbsp. onion powder

1 tbsp. garlic powder

1 tsp. ground cumin

1 tsp. oregano

1 tsp. ground thyme

Wild Game Rub

Although a great rub for venison and other wild game, this rub is equally good on almost any meat.

½ cup paprika

½ cup salt

½ cup brown sugar

1 tbsp. ground black pepper

¼ cup coarsely ground peppercorns

1 tbsp. garlic powder

1 tbsp. onion powder

1 tsp. crushed cayenne pepper

1 tsp. dried thyme

1 tbsp. juniper berries (crushed and minced)

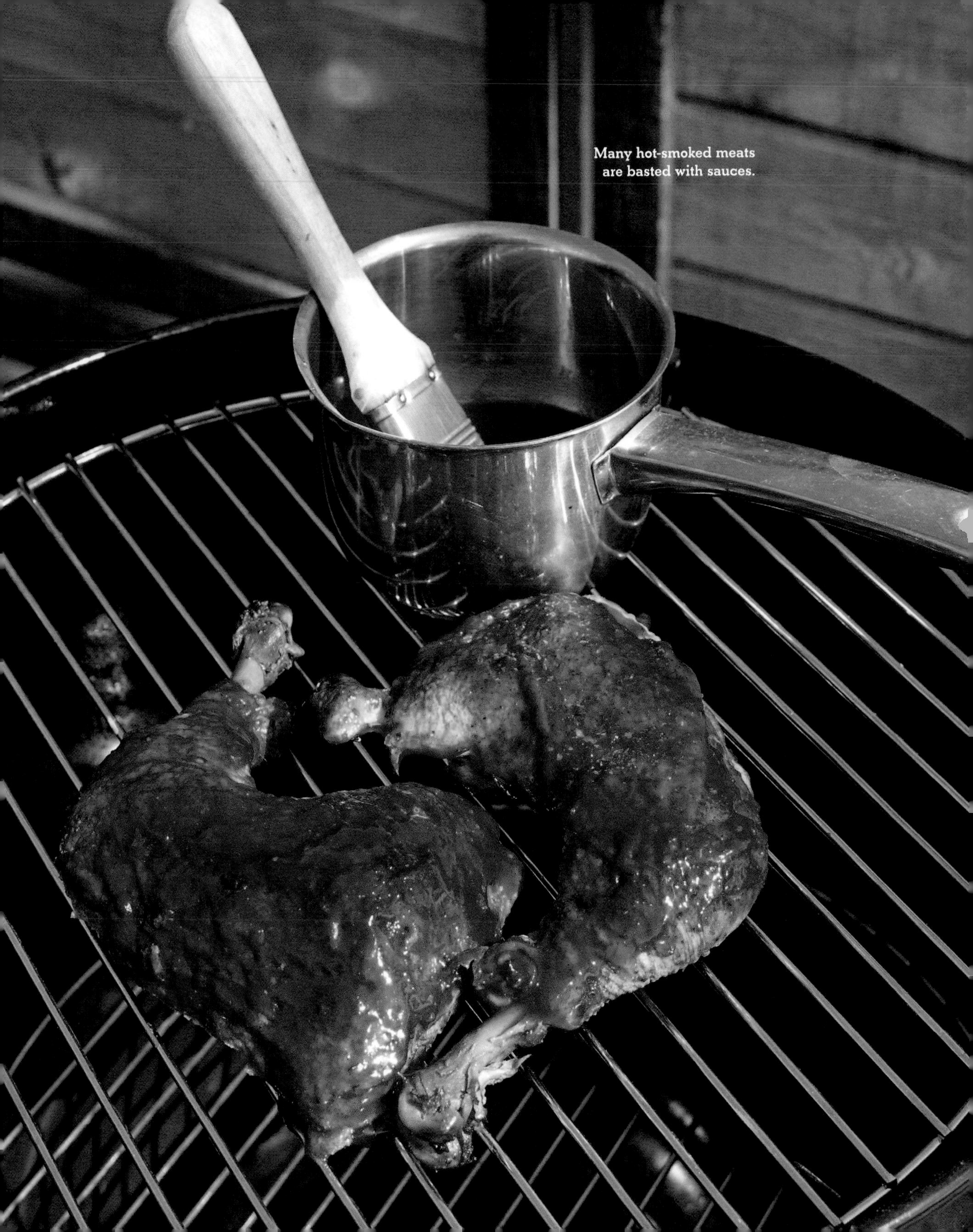

Many hot-smoked meats
are basted with sauces.

Sauces

Sauces are a major part of smoke cooking. Any number of commercial sauces, including the popular barbecue sauces, are available. You can start with ready-made sauces and doctor them to your tastes, or create your own great-tasting sauces. Sauces can be extremely simple, or they can include a multitude of herbs and spices. Some sauces do best with specific meats, although experimenting is half the fun.

To make up the sauce, place the liquids in a saucepan, add the dry ingredients, stir, and simmer until well blended. Set aside for a couple of hours to allow the flavors to mingle. Most of these sauces can be stored in the refrigerator for several days. For longer storage, place in freezer containers and freeze.

BELOW: Making up your own barbecue basting sauce is fun and easy.

Sauces can be applied before cooking and/or during the cooking process. Sauces containing oils or sugar can cause flare-ups and caking if used with direct heat. Sweet sauces are often applied in the last portion of the cooking process to prevent burned, dried exteriors. Another method is to smoke-cook for a period of time, place the meat in aluminum foil, apply the sauce, wrap tightly, and finish cooking. This is a great way of combining rubs with sauces. It provides a very tasty, smoked, but juicy meat and is my favorite method of finishing hot-smoked meats.

Easy-Does-It Sauce

1 cup ketchup	1 tsp. ground ginger
1 cup cider vinegar	1 tsp. salt
1 tbsp. brown sugar	½ tsp. cayenne pepper

This sauce can simply be mixed together with a wire whip and placed in the refrigerator to let the flavors blend.

Barbecue Beef Sauce

1 large can tomato sauce	1 tsp. freshly ground black pepper
1 small can tomato paste	1 tsp. salt
1 cup cider vinegar	1 cup finely minced onion
1 cup brown sugar	2 mashed and finely minced garlic cloves
1 tbsp. chili powder	1 tbsp. olive oil
1 tbsp. chopped basil	

Sauté the finely minced onion and garlic in the olive oil until transparent. Add the other ingredients and simmer until well blended.

Barbecue Pork Sauce

1 (24-oz.) bottle ketchup	1 large onion, minced very finely
½ cup cider vinegar	1 tbsp. olive oil
½ cup brown sugar	2 to 4 dashes Tabasco sauce
1 tsp. salt	1 tbsp. lemon pepper
2 mashed and finely minced garlic cloves	1 tsp. ground red pepper (or to taste)

Sauté the finely minced onion and garlic in the olive oil until transparent. Add other ingredients and simmer until well blended. Add the Tabasco and ground red pepper to taste.

BELOW: When using fresh onions and garlic in a sauce, cook in oil until transparent and then add the other ingredients and simmer until desired consistency is reached.

ABOVE: By using ketchup as a base, you can easily make up your own sauce.

Wild Game Barbecue Sauce

I (32-oz.) bottle ketchup

4 tbsp. cider vinegar

I tbsp. liquid smoke

I tsp. garlic powder

I tbsp. chili powder

I tbsp. dried minced onion

½ cup brown sugar

½ tsp. ground dry mustard

½ tsp. cayenne pepper

Wright's Outrageous Barbecue Sauce

3 medium onions, finely minced

3 cloves garlic, finely minced

3 tbsp. vegetable oil

3 cups ketchup

½ cup firmly packed brown sugar

⅓ cup white wine vinegar

3 tbsp. Wright's Natural Hickory Seasoning

2 tbsp. Grey Poupon Dijon mustard

I tsp. liquid hot pepper seasoning

Sauté the onions and garlic in the olive oil until transparent. Add other ingredients and simmer until well blended.

Kansas City-Style Barbecue Sauce

I small can tomato sauce

I small can tomato paste

½ cup cider vinegar

I medium onion, finely chopped

2 garlic cloves, finely minced

I tbsp. vegetable oil

3 tbsp. molasses

¼ cup firmly packed brown sugar

2 tbsp. chili powder

3 tbsp. Worcestershire sauce

I tbsp. prepared mustard

I tbsp. freshly ground black pepper

Sauté the onion and garlic in the olive oil until transparent. Add other ingredients and simmer until well blended.

Pineapple Ham Glaze

I (8-oz.) can crushed pineapple, undrained

I cup firmly packed brown sugar

I tbsp. prepared mustard

I tsp. dry mustard

2 tbsp. reconstituted lemon juice

I tsp. salt

Honey Chicken Sauce

I small can tomato sauce	I tbsp. Worcestershire sauce
½ cup cider vinegar	I tbsp. chili powder
I cup honey	I tsp. hot sauce (or to taste)
2 tbsp. reconstituted lemon juice	I½ tsp. paprika
I tsp. celery salt	I tbsp. prepared mustard
I tsp. garlic salt	

Hot Barbecue Sauce

I large can tomato sauce	I tsp. crushed red pepper
I tsp. Worcestershire sauce	I tbsp. chili powder
2 tbsp. reconstituted lemon juice	I tsp. garlic powder
I (12-oz.) bottle ketchup	I tsp. onion powder
I tsp. Louisiana hot sauce	I tsp. ground mustard
I tsp. ground red pepper	I cup beer or wine

Currant Game Sauce

½ cup wine	I jar red currant jelly
2½ tbsp. grated horseradish	Cinnamon and nutmeg to taste

Heat the jelly until soft. Blend in other ingredients. Serve over wild game meat.

Marinades

Marinades are primarily used for soaking meats prior to smoke cooking. Marinades may also be used to add flavor to the water pans when water-smoker cooking. A wide range of liquids, seasonings, and herbs can be used to create marinades. Again, you can purchase any number of premixed marinades. One of my favorite prepared mixes

ABOVE: Soaking meats in marinades, basting with marinades, or using marinades in water-pan smokers adds to the flavor.

is teriyaki marinade. We use it on venison loin steaks prior to grilling. You can also make your own marinades using a number of liquids as a base. Some marinades are also used as basting sauces. Marinades used as basting sauces, however, should be kept separate from those used to presoak the meats to prevent cross-contamination. Once you have soaked the meats in the marinade, discard it.

Marinades can also be extremely simple, or complex with lots of ingredients. Some may require cooking, others simply mixing the ingredients well. To marinate, place the meat and marinade in a noncorrosive container with a lid (or covered with plastic wrap) or plastic sealable food storage bag, and place in the refrigerator. Allow the meat to marinate for the time suggested by the recipe or anywhere from 1 hour to several hours. Always refrigerate the marinating meat. Following are some make-it-yourself marinade recipes. Start with these and experiment with your own favorite flavorings and seasonings.

Easy-Does-It Italian Marinade

1 bottle Italian salad dressing	1 tsp. onion powder
2 tbsp. lemon pepper	1 tsp. freshly ground black pepper
1 tsp. garlic powder	

Italian Marinade

¾ cup olive oil	½ tsp. salt
¾ cup red wine vinegar	1½ tsp. oregano
½ cup onion (finely chopped)	¼ tsp. pepper
1 garlic clove (crushed and finely diced)	

Oriental Marinade

¾ cup soy sauce	2 cloves garlic (finely chopped)
¼ cup pineapple juice	1 tsp. ground ginger
¼ cup lemon juice	3 tbsp. brown sugar
¼ cup cooking oil	

White Wine Marinade

1 cup white wine	½ cup cooking oil
½ cup lemon juice	1 tsp. grated lemon rind

Herb Garlic Marinade

¾ cup cooking oil	1 tsp. thyme
¾ cup red wine vinegar	1 tsp. salt
3 cloves garlic (finely minced)	½ tsp. peppercorns (freshly ground)
1 tsp. basil	

Pineapple

1 (20-oz.) can crushed pineapple, undrained	1 tbsp. Worcestershire sauce
1 cup red wine vinegar	1 tsp. thyme
½ cup onion (finely chopped)	½ tsp. salt
	½ tsp. pepper

(12)

Recipes for Hot Smoking

HOT SMOKING, OR cooking meats with the addition of smoke, provides delicious fare of almost any kind of meat—including beef, pork, poultry, fish, and game. Following are some of our favorite recipes you might want to try. Some are slow cooking with indirect heat, some are flash cooking with direct heat, but the main ingredient in all is the use of smoke for added flavoring.

Pork Ribs

Pork ribs are one of the favored hot-smoked meats. Contests are held all across the country to see who produces the best hot-smoked ribs. The meat chosen and the preparation, the rubs and sauces used, as well as the smoking methods all contribute to the successful result. Smoke-cooking ribs, however, is an easy-does-it backyard cooking project that can be done with a charcoal, electric, water pan, indirect-heat wood smoker, or even a large covered barbecue grill. The main keys to succulent ribs are low heat and a long cooking time.

A whole pork rib slab consists of several parts, including the ribs, the cartilage (also called the brisket), the sternum, point, the skirt, and the fell or membrane. Whole ribs may be cooked as the whole slab, but are more commonly divided into the spareribs (bottom section) and the back ribs (those coming from the top part of the

ABOVE: Pork ribs are some of the most popular hot-smoked meats. When I smoke, I usually load the smoker full. Shown are ribs and chicken.

rib cage), along the backbone or loin area. If the back rib slabs weigh under 1 ¾ pounds, they are usually called "baby back" ribs and are one of the most expensive pork cuts. You can purchase whole slabs, spareribs, or back ribs. Other than the pigs we butcher, I prefer to purchase whole slabs and cut the baby backs, as well as the bottom sternum cartilage, off myself. I normally, however, smoke all at the same time. One of the most important preparations you can do is remove the membrane on the back of the ribs.

Not only is it tough, but it prevents the seasonings, sauce, and smoke from penetrating into the meat. The membrane is not easy to remove. Use a dull table knife to pry up an edge, and then grasp the membrane with a paper towel and pull it off. It will normally come off

Rib parts

Back Ribs

Spare Ribs

Sterum (Briskat)

ABOVE: A rib slab consists of several parts.

in several pieces. I use a pair of catfish skinning pliers, available at sporting goods stores. These pliers have small sharp gripping edges that easily grasp the membrane and make it easy to remove.

The next step is to apply a dry rub to the ribs, front and back. Set aside in a cool place for about an hour, and then place in the smoker. My method for the wood smoker is to smoke at 225°F for an hour or so, remove the ribs, apply barbecue sauce, and wrap tightly in aluminum foil. Continue smoking at 225°F until the ribs are done. Some prefer to continue smoking in the smoker without the aluminum foil wrap, until the ribs are done, basting for the last 30 minutes with sauce.

Boston Butt Pulled Pork

Another favorite pork recipe is pulled pork. This is most commonly made from the pork picnic roast, pork shoulder, or Boston butt pork cut; and the amount of fat and meat, along with the bone inside, creates just the right type and amount of meat for slow smoke cooking. This is one of the more economical cuts of meat and is an ideal meat for slow cooking in a charcoal-fired water-pan cooker. It takes time to slow-cook a pork roast. An excellent recipe comes with the Brinkmann smoker.

Score the pork roast and then rub evenly with garlic powder, coarse black pepper, and paprika. Brush the roast lightly with Worcestershire sauce. Wrap the roast in foil and refrigerate overnight. Place ¼ cup red wine in the water pan and fill the remainder with water. Cook about 45 to 60 minutes per pound, depending on thickness of the roast. A good wood chip to use is cherry. Wrap in aluminum foil for the last hour or so.

Smoked Pork Picnic Roast

A whole pork shoulder, also often called a picnic shoulder or picnic roast, is a pork roast that is not only economical but is the perfect smoking cut. It can be served as is or as a pulled-pork dish and is one of our favorite pork dishes. This is an excellent choice for dedicated indirect smokers, as a long, slow cooking time makes the meat falling off the bone tender, and juicy. This smoked meat is a traditional Southern delight. Prepare the meat by removing any skin and cutting away excess fat. Leave about a half inch of fat, you need some fat. Liberally apply the dry rub below all over the roast. Wrap in plastic and allow to sit for about an hour in refrigeration.

2 tbsp. salt	1 tbsp. black pepper
2 tbsp. paprika	1 tsp. onion powder
1 tbsp. chili powder	1 tsp. garlic powder

Preheat the smoker using the traditional hickory chips for smoke. The key to a tender, juicy roast is low and slow cooking, at 200°F to 225°F. This is basically an all-day affair, as it will take about 1 to 1 ½ hours per pound of meat. Bring the smoker up to a low temperature of 200°F. Place the shoulder in the smoker, fat-side up. Cook for 4 hours or so at low temperature and then increase the temperature to 225°F and continue to smoke-cook. After 2 more hours, baste the roast once an hour with a good vinegar-based barbecue sauce, such as the pork barbecue sauce recipe in the previous chapter.

ABOVE: A pork roast either served whole or as pulled pork is another all-time-favorite hot-smoked food.

Check the internal temperature. Once the internal temperature reaches 190°F, it's time for a fork test. Push a fork into the roast and twist. If some force is required to tear the meat, it's ready for slicing, but not quite ready to "pull." Continue to cook. Once the fork twists easily in the roast, the meat will shred easily for pulled pork.

Remove the roast from the smoker. Wrap it with 2 layers of heavy-duty aluminum foil, then a couple of heavy towels, and allow it to sit for about an hour. Shred the meat with a pair of forks, removing the bone, fat, and any gristle. Serve with additional sauce on the side.

Beer-Butt Chicken

Whole chickens smoked in this manner are a favorite at our house. We've been preparing beer-butt chicken a long time, long before there were specially made racks to hold the chicken and beer can upright, although I've never had a problem. You also don't have to use beer. Soda pop will work just as well. We've found root beer to be an excellent choice. The liquid in the can provides a simple form of "water smoking." This method can be used in a covered barbecue grill with indirect heat or in a smoker.

Cut away all excess fat from a whole fryer under 3 pounds. Remove the innards that may be packed inside the chicken and place them in an aluminum foil pouch to cook separately. Apply a dry rub to the chicken. A good choice is the simple rub in the previous chapter. It doesn't overpower the more delicate chicken meat. Cook in a smoker at 225°F for 1 hour using hickory, pecan, or cherry chips. After 1 hour, remove the chicken from the smoker, place on a piece of heavy-duty aluminum foil, and baste with barbecue sauce. The honey chicken sauce from the previous chapter is our favorite. Continue to smoke-cook at 225°F until the internal temperature of the chicken reaches 165°F. Incidentally, after the internal temperature reaches 150°F, meats will take up very little smoke flavor. You can continue cooking in the smoker or place the chicken in a 225°F to 250°F oven to finish cooking.

Bacon-Wrapped Deer Loins

Whole, slow-smoked deer loins are an excellent delicacy and a great way of using up excess venison, often the case these days with liberal deer seasons. These bacon-wrapped loins can be served hot with barbecue sauce or cold, and as thin slices for sandwiches or hors d'oeuvres with a horseradish sauce on the side. The first step is to prepare the loin. Remove the back-fat strip as well as the sinew. To remove this, start a sharp, thin knife between the sinew and meat. Then place the loin sinew-side down on a flat surface and slide the knife between the two until they are separated. Apply a rub, such as the spicy rub. Wrap bacon strips around the loin, pinning in place

ABOVE: Beer-butt chicken is a fun and delicious way to serve smoked chicken.

with toothpicks. Place the loin in the smoker and smoke at 225°F. After 2 hours, remove, pull out the toothpicks, and apply a barbecue sauce, such as the wild game sauce. Wrap the loin in heavy-duty aluminum foil and continue smoking at 225°F. Venison is best if not overcooked, so cook to no more than 160°F internally. This should take about another 2 to 3 hours. Remove, slice, and serve with additional barbecue sauce immediately for a hot dish.

Pineapple Ham

A regular, or short-cut, ham is also an excellent choice for smoking. This Polynesian-style recipe is a tradition, and the addition of smoke to the cooking adds even more flavor. Use a mild wood, such as cherry or apple, for the smoke. You can smoke-cook the ham using the traditional spit-on-a-grill or in an indirect-heat dedicated smoker.

In either case, trim up the ham, removing all but about ½ inch of fat. Score the fat, creating crisscross cuts, and then weigh it. Place in a smoker or large covered grill with rotisserie, and smoke-cook at 200°F to 225°F. If using a grill, place the wood chips in an aluminum foil pouch over the flames. Cooking time will be about 1 hour per pound of ham, but this will vary. Cook until the internal temperature is 160°F. Baste frequently during the last half hour with a pineapple sauce, such as the pineapple ham glaze.

Horizon Smoked Turkey

The Horizon Smoker folks have a good recipe for smoked turkey. This is also an excellent recipe for a turkey breast if you want to start with something less daunting.

Remove innards and place in a foil pouch for cooking separately. Rub the turkey with oil. They suggest olive oil or the olive oil cooking spray. Then apply a rub. A good choice is the simple rub (see recipe). Place the turkey or turkey breast and 1 stick of butter in a foil pan. Lay a piece of foil over the turkey. Don't seal the pan completely, just tent the turkey. Smoke the turkey, using a mild wood such as pecan, at 175°F to 200°F for 1 hour for each pound of weight. Baste every 3 hours with butter drippings from the bottom of the pan.

Beef Brisket Party

A beef brisket provides the ideal smoked meat for a party. Not only is the meat an economical cut, but it comes in big sizes and is easy to smoke. Use only a trimmed brisket, but it should still have some fat on it in order to smoke properly. Coat the brisket with a dry rub. Place on oiled racks in the smoker and smoke with hickory chips or chunks at 225°F for about an hour. Remove from the smoker, coat

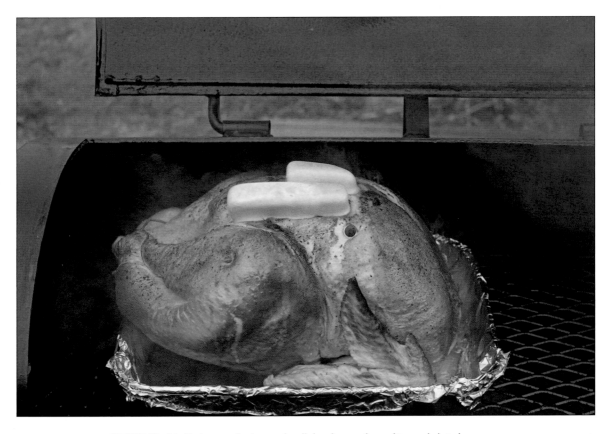

ABOVE: The big Horizon smoker is great for all-day slow smoke-cooking a whole turkey.

well with barbecue sauce, wrap in heavy-duty aluminum foil, and place the foil-wrapped brisket in a pan. Return to the smoker and smoke for 5 to 6 more hours.

Remove, pour off the liquid, and place in the refrigerator overnight. Thin-slice while chilled, remove any excess fat, and repackage in a pan tightly covered with aluminum foil. The day of the party, put back on the smoker about an hour before. The aroma of the smoke and cooking meat adds to the "flavor" of the party. Serve with buns and lots more barbecue sauce. If the party is more than a couple of days away, freeze the sliced brisket.

ABOVE: A beef brisket is one of the most economical meat cuts to smoke. Smoked brisket is great to serve for any get-together.

Hot-Smoked Panfish

Perch, bluegills, and especially white bass can be a delicious treat hot-smoked. Fish typically flakes and falls apart when hot smoking. One trick to solve the problem is to scale the fish, but leave the skin on. Cut the fish and remove head, tail, and rib cage. Or fillet the fish, leaving the skin on one side but removing the rib cage. Pour the following marinade in a plastic food container and place the fish flesh-side down in a single layer in the marinade. Cover with plastic food wrap. Allow the fish to marinate in a refrigerator for about four hours.

2 cups dry white wine	I tbsp. Worcestershire sauce
5 tbsp. crushed tarragon	½ tsp. ground red pepper (to taste or optional)
I tsp. onion powder	
I tsp. garlic powder	

Remove from the marinade and place on paper towels for about a half hour before cooking. Start the fire and add wood chips, such as cherry or mesquite. Sprinkle the fish with lemon pepper and salt to taste. Spray the grate with cooking oil and place the fish pieces skin-side down on a hot fire. Cook until the meat flakes, usually about 10 to 12 minutes. Remove from the grill with a spatula. The skin will prevent the fish from sticking to the grill. Using a sharp fillet knife, remove the skin, starting at the tail. Serve with a lemon juice and drawn butter accompaniment.

HOGS, SLOW-COOKED WITH smoke, or as it's often
called, "barbecuing," is a tradition in many parts of the country. In
the South, it's also called "pig picking," because friends, neighbors,
even whole communities are invited to share in the delicious, succulent pork, picking pieces off the carcass and eating by hand. A whole
roasted hog, done in the old-fashioned way, is indeed a tasty treat. Pig
picking is also where the term "close to the bone" comes from, as the
best-tasting roasted pork is next to the ribs and backbone. Roasting a

13
The Ultimate Smoking Experience

whole hog takes patience, and a lot of time. It also takes a bit of experience, but it's a fun event everyone can enjoy.

I had a neighbor who really enjoyed whole-hog roasting. He also made his own wine, and even occasionally showed up with a glass jar of clear but potent homemade product. Sipping and smoking went together as far as he was concerned, especially since it took all night. Whole hog roasting can be done in two methods, including cutting up the pig and cooking the sections, but the tradition is to cook the entire pig whole, but split down the middle depending on size.

For this method, it's important to have the right pig. A pig weighing between 90 and 100 pounds is about the right size. Smaller pigs from 60 to 80 pounds are also great for whole hog roasting. Anything larger and there's too much fat covering the carcass. The excess fat is more likely to burn rather than the meat cooking slowly and evenly. The pig should be killed, dressed, and properly chilled to 40°F the day before you begin cooking.

Whole hog roasting can be done using several means. If you have a big wood smoker capable of doing a whole hog, you're way ahead of most. Those that frequently do whole-hog roasts usually construct special smokers for the job. They are sometimes constructed of concrete blocks and lined with firebrick. Large welded grates are used to hold the hog halves. Some hog roasters have also constructed spits that can be turned to roast the hogs more evenly, but it's really not necessary.

If the pig picking is to take place around 4:30 to 5:00 in the afternoon, the fire is started in the pit smoker about 10:00 the night before. Bags of charcoal, fueled with green hickory logs to create the

BELOW: A pit barbecue can feed a crowd, but it takes work.

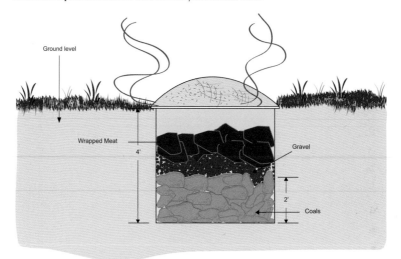

smoke, are started. You'll need a layer of coals about 2 feet thick. In a couple of hours, or around midnight, the fire should be about right. The grates are laid in place, and the hog halves are wired to metal support bars. The hog halves are then placed over the fire skin-side up. You'd better have lots of lawn chairs, because it's a continual job of tending the fire. Part of what makes whole roast hog so delicious is the slow, low fire. Ideally, the fire temperature should be kept around 180°F. After about 7 to 8 hours, the fat will begin to bubble through the skin. The pig is carefully turned over with the skin-side down, and basting with a homemade barbecue sauce begins.

When the slow-roasted, slow-smoked pig is done, cut one half from the bone. Mix the pieces well together and serve with sauce on the side. Then carefully slide the other half of the pig onto a clean board or picnic table for the "pig picking," and stand back. Have plenty of big napkins on hand because it's finger-licking good.

Pit barbecuing, or earth roasting, is another great way of slow smoke-cooking meats. Several years ago, Kansas invited a number of outdoor writers to an event that includes pit-roasting a Kansas buffalo. It was some of the most scrumptious meat I've ever tasted. Pit or earth roasting is done using nothing more than a deeply dug pit. I can't pit-roast on my place in the Ozarks because we can't dig that deep without dynamite. In any case, dig a pit about 4 feet deep and large enough to hold the amount of meat you intend to cook. A pit 4 feet wide and 6 feet long will hold about a hindquarter or 2, depending on size, or 4 large rib racks. Using hardwood logs that have dried for at least a year, build a roaring fire in the bottom of the pit. Keep adding to the fire until you have a 2-foot layer of coals. This will take 12 to 14 hours.

Either pork or beef can be used for the roast. Beef is traditional. Some say the origin of barbecuing in the United States came from this method used in the West by ranchers to feed their cowboys. Several days before you intend to roast, acquire or cut up the beef. If using rib racks, cut them into 6 or 8 rib sizes. Cut the hindquarter into evenly sized chunks. Remove excess exterior fat. For a really meaty, tasty treat, many earth-roast chefs use sirloin tip roasts. Season with salt and pepper and then wrap in two layers of cheesecloth.

Wrap the bundles with burlap and tie with twine. Chill until it's time to begin cooking. Another method is to drizzle sauce over the meat, then place it in brown paper bags and then wrap in burlap. Some like to tie the burlap with light-duty wire. Baling wire was the choice in the old days. In this method, the chilled meat is wrapped just before it is placed on the coals, as the sauce will seep through the bag.

When you're ready to cook, about 10 to 12 hours before you intend to serve, place a 1- to 2-inch layer of clean gravel on the 2-foot bed of hot coals. Use a rake to tamp and pack the gravel, but be careful—it's hot. Lay steel pipes across the pit and place a sheet of plywood over them. A sheet of metal like barn siding is also often used. Shovel soil over the metal or plywood cover, making sure you have formed a good seal, although a little air slipping out will help prevent the fire from

BELOW: You'll also need lots of sauce, but it's easy to make up your own.

going out. Then just go about your business of getting ready for your guests. After about 8 hours of cooking, using leather gloves, unearth the pit and pull out the meat packages. If the meat hasn't been presoaked with sauce, unwrap, cut into serving-size pieces, and add sauce. If the meat was cooked with sauce, cut into serving-size pieces and present sauce on the side.

You'll need lots of sauce, and the following beef barbecue sauce recipe takes up a large pan. Double or triple the recipe if you need more.

2 cups chopped onion	I tsp. ground red pepper
4 garlic cloves, smashed and finely diced	2 tbsp. chili powder
½ cup cooking oil	2 tbsp. steak sauce
4 cups ketchup	2 tbsp. Worcestershire sauce
I cup vinegar	2 tbsp. prepared mustard
I tsp. ground celery seed	I cup brown sugar
I tsp. cumin powder	½ cup blackstrap molasses
I tsp. salt	

In a large saucepan, cook the onions and garlic in the oil until transparent. Add the ketchup, vinegar, and spices and cook to desired consistency, adding the brown sugar and molasses toward the last.

Index

NOTES